Interpreting Social Change

in America

DATE DUE			

Studies in Sociology

Interpreting Social Change in America

By NORMAN F. WASHBURNE

RANDOM HOUSE

New York

Dedicated to
Mr. Irwin Stein of Scarsdale, New York,
who was my closest friend as an undergraduate at the University of Missouri
and who originally interested me in sociology as a field
and in social change as a specific focus

LIBRARY OF CONGRESS CATALOG CARD NUMBER: 54-10158
MANUFACTURED IN THE UNITED STATES OF AMERICA

Editor's Foreword

In recent years sociology in the United States has been occupied in large measure with investigation of social structure and social organization. An enormous body of research, part of it informed by systematic theory and marked by methodological sophistication, centers around social stratification, large-scale organizations, and the structure of small groups. Some writers have assigned a priority to this preoccupation, most explicitly certain exponents of "structural-functional" theory. And introductory textbooks more often than not in their coverage stress pattern, structure, organization, persistencies, giving short shrift to change and disorganization in society—treating these matters, it sometimes seems, as residual or secondary concerns.

This situation provokes uneasiness in various quarters, including sociological circles; it has even induced at times the charge of conservative bias. Yet most sociologists, including several of those thus charged, agree in principle that the questions of the *how* and *why* of change are as central a task as the *how* and *why* of persistence and pattern in the sociocultural world. In the final analysis—which of course is never final—the two tasks merge into one. This point of view, it may be claimed, is the underlying lesson of this study.

Professor Washburne would be the first, I know, to deny that his work pushes deeply into the theoretical problem of the relation between structure and change. But he has written a valuable introduction to this problem, which is clarified especially by his careful and consistent treatment of the institutional structure as a dynamic equilibrium. Moreover, he brings out, in unique juxtaposition—but in a manner meaningful for the neophyte of sociological study—interconnections among institutional functions, social processes, and social movements. His discussion of these concepts and of relevant concrete materials is clear and straightforward. It is also enriched by judicious use of leads drawn from such seminal contributors to social theory as Max Weber and Karl Mannheim.

Finally, the analysis of change developed in the earlier chapters is applied to the current American scene. Professor Washburne underscores the conspicuous trends of urbanization and bureaucratization and illustrates the far-reaching influence of these trends with succinct depictions of changes in family life, government and economy, science and education, religion and recreation. No one of these institutional areas, as the author emphasizes, can be developed fully in a work of this size. Nor can the complex problems of social change be analyzed thoroughly. This study, however, as an introduction to these problems, provides the reader a suggestive scheme of interpretation. The study should, I believe, also be an inducement to examine further the crucial but frequently neglected dynamic nature of the social order.

CHARLES H. PAGE.

Acknowledgments

It is, of course, impossible to acknowledge all intellectual debts, because they are too numerous. However, for their specific help in the preparation of this work, I wish to thank my wife who had to take up the slack at home while I wrote; President Dolph Camp and Dean Robert J. Kibbee of Southern State College for reducing my teaching load and providing me with secretarial assistance; Professors Stanley R. Rolnick and William Brueckheimer of the Division of Social Science of Southern State College for their helpful criticism of the manuscript; and Professor Charles H. Page, the general editor of this series, whose suggestions have been invaluable. I am particularly grateful to Miss Janette Crumpler for her skilful preparation of the manuscript. This work could not have been completed without the help of these and many other people, but they are in no way responsible for any of its shortcomings.

Contents

Introduction

We know of no society that does not change during the course of its history. Even the most casual observations of the way people live on this earth lead to the feeling that change is somehow written into the nature of human beings, both as individuals and as societies.

Americans are particularly cognizant of social change. Those who are in their fifties have watched the world into which they were born virtually drop from under them as a new world has been built about them during the course of their lives. They have witnessed amazing changes in the things they use, the way they use them, and in the reasons they use them the way they do.

Every school child is aware of the fabulous changes in technology which have occurred in the last fifty years. Machines and gadgets which are commonplace today were figments of the imagination of the "idle dreamers" of yesteryear. Those of us who have gone through civil defense drills designed to protect us from atomic bomb attack find somewhat amusing, if ironically so, the terror experienced by the citizens of Europe when during World War I they were threatened with aerial bombs which seem to us today to be something like overgrown hand grenades. We enjoy reading advertisements in the magazines of the early 1900s with the quaint costumes and funny little automobiles. We are similarly amused by the turn-of-the-century concept of the airplane as an elaborate kite, a toy for rich playboys. In the very recent past we have experienced the growth of television as a whole new industry, and sometimes we reflect upon the speed with which we have come to regard it as essential to our lives.

Most Americans are also aware of change in the problems which face them. There have been changes in political and economic structure, marriage, recreation, and many other areas of our social organization. Prohibition and repeal, depression and inflation, war, peace, and police action have flashed through the American's consciousness in a never-ending succession of headlines, crises, and upsets. We are alarmed at our growing divorce rate. We have seen the political breakdown of the "solid South" in at least two elections. We have witnessed the phenomenal growth of governmental bureaucracy and of the bureaucracies of giant industries. We have seen the labor unions grow from the organizations of a few radicals to colossal structures which carry immense political weight in our nation.

Therefore, the statement that society is changing seems to most of us as trite and as obvious as did the remark, "My, how you've grown!" which greeted us with the visit of every relative and friend of the family while we were children. Of course we had grown; what else could we do? And of course society is changing.

But the reasons for social change are not as obvious as the reasons for individual growth. All problems of individual maturation have by no means been solved by the biologists, physiologists, and psychologists studying them; but at least we can say certainly that the growth of the individual is an inevitable biological and psychological function, and that we understand many of the mechanisms of growth. It is the purpose of this study to try to gain a similar understanding of the reasons for and the mechanisms of social change.

We also know the direction of individual growth: one grows up as one gets older; one becomes more mature. Unless there are degenerative processes set in motion by some pathological condition, the direction of growth in the individual is inevitable. However, we are not so certain about the direction of social change. True, in the United States we seem to be committed to a belief in inevitable progress, and we seem to produce unendingly more, and perhaps better, gadgets; but while many have hailed the first half of the twentieth century as the dawn of a new era, for others the death of old forms of life has brought disaster, and the rapid changes have left them bewildered and hurt. Even though Americans have been brought up to believe in continual progress, with the conviction that the world is getting better, many of them have extreme doubts as to the wisdom of many of the changes that have taken place. Many Americans have felt that the changes are far from progressive, but are instead rather chaotic in nature, make no sense, actually have no direction. Everyone has had to react to changes in some way, and each of us has had constantly to readjust his way of life and very often even the basic values by which he lives. Sometimes these readjustments are pleasant; sometimes they are unpleasant. But readjust we must.

Does change in America have a direction? If so, what is it, and is it likely to continue in the future? Can we plan for it? Can we make ourselves ready for the adjustments that must come, or do we constantly run the chance of disaster, of losing all that each of us has worked for? These also are questions that this study will investigate.

Of course, one cannot deal, especially in a short work, with every possible type of change and with every changing fact of life. The scope of the inquiry must be limited. So we shall be concerned primarily with major changes in the basic things we use to help us live, the way we use those things, and in our reasons for using them the way we do. We shall not deal at any great length with fads, with new gadgets which have relatively little to do with our fundamental way of life, with changes in the personnel of our businesses, our politics, or our churches, or with changes in social phenomena which do not seem to have far-reaching effects upon our way of life.

In other words, we shall be considering those basic social and cultural changes in the United States which have made life today markedly different from life fifty years ago and which are likely to make life in the future markedly different from life today. Our method of analysis will be to discuss these significant changes in terms of the broad divisions of society and culture which they affect most greatly. In particular, we shall analyze the major changes which have taken place in the American family, governmental system, the economic system, and in the religious, scientific, recreational, and educational aspects of American life. We shall be interested in how changes in each of these areas of our society and culture affect the other areas, and in how these changes affect the life of individual Americans in their interaction with their fellow citizens.

Chapter One presents the social institution as a unit of change and attempts to show why and how institutional changes affect the daily life of citizens of our society. The second chapter discusses the reasons social institutions change. The third chapter explains how social institutions change, and the final chapter deals with the major directions of change today in the major social institutions in American society.

chapter one

The Social Institution
as the Unit of Change

The Functions of Culture and Social Organization

The changes that are important to people are those which affect the efficiency of the fulfilment of the functions of our culture and our social organization. Therefore, in order to analyze social change it is necessary to depict those functions.

Basically human culture and social organization exist in order to meet man's needs. All living things have certain biological needs which must be met if they are to stay alive as individuals and as species. Among these are the need for food, protection, and reproduction. All animals, indeed all living things, must adapt themselves to their environment. They must take from their environment the things which they need to maintain life, and they must prevent hostile forces in their environment from exterminating their life.

Most other mammals—man's nearest relatives among animals—are hereditarily equipped with special talents, skills, and instincts which enable them to meet their basic needs, to adapt themselves to their environment. Most mammals are highly specialized; that is, each species has characteristics which enable it to maintain its existence in a world which is at least partially hostile. For instance, the fox is swift of foot and can detect odors and sounds with great acuteness; the cat is also swift and has instinctive ability to make use of cover and camouflage in stalking its prey; the rabbit would never have become the ubiquitous rodent it is were it not for its ability to reproduce itself in great enough numbers to withstand the ravages of nearly every carnivorous animal. All species without the requisite speed, acuity of senses, instinctual skills, reproductive ability, or protective size and coloration have long since perished from this earth—except man.

Man is neither particularly fast nor strong, nor are his senses particularly acute, nor do his size and coloration lend themselves to easy camouflage. He cannot reproduce himself rapidly, for it takes a long time for him to create a child and a longer time to raise it to the point where it can take care of itself. But man does have the capacity to invent and learn language, which in turn enables him to build a culture and to organize society.

Other animals are hereditarily adapted to their environment, but man, by means of his culture and his social organization, changes his environment to suit himself. He cannot grow fur to keep himself warm, but he can and does weave cloth to make clothing and he can and does distribute clothing. He does not have the ability to leap three times his own height, as do some animals, nor does he have teeth which he can effectively use to kill and eat wild game. But he has learned to manufacture and to share tools and weapons which allow him to compensate for these lacks—and much more. Briefly then, man uses his culture and his social organization to keep himself alive, to adapt his environment to his needs, and to protect himself from those aspects of his environment which are hostile to him. It may therefore be said that the primary function of culture and of social organization is the meeting of man's basic needs.

However, the primary function is not the only function of man's culture and social organization, for man has needs other than basic ones. He has needs which may be derived from the way he meets his basic needs. There are, for example, a number of derived human needs associated with man's use of language. Human beings are not born with the use of language. An individual isolated from society from birth does not develop language on his own. However, most men must be able to talk; and in complex civilizations most men also must be able to read and to write in order to participate in the culture and the social organization which they use to meet their basic biological needs. Hence there is the need for an educative process whereby children learn language. In civilizations there is the additional need for inexpensive, widely distributed writing materials, and so on. These needs are derived human needs. A very significant proportion of the functions of culture and social organization is involved in the meeting of derived human needs, as well as basic human needs.

Not only can human needs be divided into those which are basic and others which are derived, but they can also be classified according to the degree to which they are widespread. Some needs, such as the need to eat, are common to all people and can be called universal needs. On the other hand, some needs apply only to some people. For instance, some people seem to feel the need to excel at whatever they do, while others evidently do not feel this need. Those needs which apply only to some people may be called particular needs.

Human needs may also be classified according to whether they are needs of the society as a whole, of individuals within the society, or of groups of individuals within the society. The needs of the society as a whole are sometimes called societal needs. Among them are the needs that must be met if society is to exist. For instance, the need for the reproduction of the species is a basic societal need, as is the need for integration of social elements into a functioning whole. Associated with many societal needs are individual needs, both universal and particular in nature. For example, associated with the societal need for the reproduction of the species are the universal individual needs for sexual gratification, companionship, and affection.

One of the particular needs of some individuals is associated with the societal need for an established authority. Clearly, if men are to pull together to help each other stay comfortable and alive, there must be some

established authority - government - without it's
anarchy

leadership and direction; so there is undoubtedly a societal need for an established authority. Associated with it is the need of some few individuals within the society to wield power and to provide the leadership and direction that society must have. Since not all individuals feel this need, and since some do, the need for satisfaction of a power drive may be classified as a particular individual need.

The individuals of any society are organized into various groups, and there is reason to believe that there are needs which are experienced by those groups. For instance, any group must have some kind of symbol of identification if it is to have any continuity. Formally organized groups (for example, lodges, corporations, schools) have charters, names, and rituals which provide this identification. Informal groups (for example, friendship groups, cliques, gangs) have private jokes, an argot, and perhaps an established routine of activity which serve the same function. Therefore the need for such an identifying symbol might be classed as a universal group need. An example of a particular group need, on the other hand, is the requirement of a political machine to win elections, at least occasionally, if it is to remain in active existence. This need is experienced only by those groups engaged in a certain kind of political activity and hence is classified as particular in nature.

The Unit of Study

The problem to which this study is addressed is that of discovering and analyzing the mechanisms and the direction of change in the way the culture and the social organization of America meet the basic and derived, the universal and particular needs of the individuals and groups within American society as well as the needs of the society as a whole.

Some sociologists, in attacking this problem, attempt to distinguish between changes in social organization and changes in culture. They believe that social change involves only the study of changes in social organization; that is, they feel that the study of social change is limited to those changes that take place in social structures, group relationships, status configurations, and the like. They indicate that the study of cultural change, on the other hand, should deal with changes in technology, modes of behavior, attitudes, ways of thinking, doing, and feeling, and so forth.

The distinction between society and culture is often a useful one. But in approaching the problem of change this distinction is not fruitful because both change in social organization and change in culture involve changes in man's approach to meeting his needs; and change in one is dependent upon change in the other. Authors who claim to deal only with cultural change find that they must account for cultural changes partially in terms of changes which take place in social organization.

It would be difficult, for example, to account for many changes which have taken place in the social organization of our economic system without understanding changes that have taken place in our material culture and in the folkways and mores associated with them. Is it possible to account for industrial unionism without understanding the technological development of mass industry and without taking account of the modification of the American ideals of individualism involved?

Difference between society and culture?

We use, therefore, a unit of analysis which will enable us to deal with both changes in social organization and changes in culture, with particular reference to the way such changes affect the way our needs are met. This unit of analysis is the social institution.

Social Institutions as Analytical Units

Man's needs are manifested in interrelated clusters. For instance, the fulfilment of some of man's needs is related to his use of the materials he finds on earth and to the necessity of converting those materials into readily usable form. With the possible exception of life in the Garden of Eden, man has always had to work for a living and a whole group of human needs cluster about this fact. "Getting a living" can be therefore called a basic problem of human life. In meeting the needs associated with the problem of getting a living, man has certain materials with which to work. These are the raw materials that he finds in his natural environment. In order to solve the problem of getting a living, he has had to modify those materials to convert them into usable form. The results of the process of the modification of raw materials are called artifacts or, simply, man-made things. Now except in the rare instance of direct and original invention, the manufacture of an artifact is possible only when man has the requisite skill to use and fashion his raw materials. Furthermore, unless the artifact he produces is very simple, he needs to have other artifacts called *tools* to help him with his work.

In complex societies, in which men are specialists rather than jacks-of-all-trades, the products of the use of skills and tools must be distributed among the population. In addition to the skills and the tools of production, there must exist techniques and tools for the distribution of products. And there must also exist social organizations and groups dedicated to the various tasks of both production and distribution.

Skills, techniques, social organization, and artifacts then are associated with the solution to the problem of getting a living. This problem also involves a pattern of values. Values determine what is good, what is bad, better, and worse, what is right and wrong among alternatives men face. There are many courses men can take in the process of getting a living, one of them being the practice of taking the living from those who have it already, not bothering to work for it themselves. The fact that most men do not follow this course is due in large measure to the general belief among people that it is wrong to steal from others. This belief is part of our value system. Similarly, men must make decisions about what kinds of things they want and what they are willing to give up for them. Usually, men are not able to have everything they want; they live in a world of scarcity. Therefore the relative worth of various goods must be decided. These decisions are also determined by the value system of the society.

The pattern of values, tools, skills, techniques, and social organization which functions to solve the basic problem of getting a living constitutes the social institution which is known as the economic system.

Human needs are associated with several other basic problems of life. For example, wherever society exists, man must set up lines of authority for the purpose of organizing for the common defense, the administration of justice, and the preservation of domestic order. The artifacts, skills, techniques, attitudes, values, and patterns of social organization which evolve to meet the human needs associated with this basic problem make up the social institution of government.

Similarly, the artifacts, skills, techniques, attitudes, values, and patterns of social organization which serve the needs associated with the reproduction of the species constitute the social institution of the family. Those which meet the needs related to the problem of training children for their roles as adults constitute the social institution we call the educational system. Those which serve the needs associated with the problems of breaking routine, relaxing, and experiencing enjoyment are represented in the institution of recreation. Those which meet the needs involved in the problems of understanding the meaning of life, death, man's destiny, and of dealing with the supernatural constitute the social institution of religion. And those which function to meet needs related to the problem of increasing man's store of skills and knowledge make up the institution of science. There are, of course, other basic problems of human life, and hence other social institutions. But these are among the most important and are those with which we will deal.

The concept of social institution, as we have used the term, includes the following interrelated components:

1. *Human needs*, which include societal, group, and individual needs which may be basic or derived, universal or particular in nature. These human needs are associated with basic problems of life.

2. *Basic problems of human life*, which are those problems which man must solve if he is to live and prosper.

3. *Artifacts*, or man-made things. These include every modification of natural environment that man has achieved. Taken *en masse* they are sometimes called *material culture*.

4. *Skills and techniques*, which are normal ways of doing things. That is, skills and techniques are learned by individuals within a culture as the proper ways of accomplishing goals, and the members of a given society or group tend to share skills and techniques in common.

5. *Attitudes and values*, which are, essentially, the normal ways people think and feel. That is, attitudes and values are transmitted to individuals by the people they associate with most closely, and members of a given society or group tend to share their attitudes and values in common.

6. *Patterns of social organization*, which are the typical ways people group themselves and stratify themselves in their solutions of the basic problems of life.

If the term *folkway* is defined as a normal way of doing, thinking, or feeling and if the term *mores* is defined as folkways which are regarded by societies as especially important, so significant that the people of the society feel threatened if one of their number breaks them, then skills, techniques, attitudes and values (4 and 5 above) may be incorporated into the well-known phrase *folkways and mores*. A social institution formally defined, then, is a group of folkways, mores, and artifacts which together with a pattern of social organization serve the human needs associated with a basic problem of human life.[1]

Of the different components of a social institution, only the basic problem of life which it solves, and some of the human needs associated with that problem, are common to all men in all societies. Institutions differ from society to society and from time to time in the same society in the folkways, mores, artifacts, and patterns of social organization of which they are composed. Many of the derived human needs which the institutions serve also vary from society to society and from time to time within the same society.

Indeed, the sociologically significant differences between any two societies are the differences that exist in their institutional structures. These differences are reviewed in detail in lectures and books about comparative religion, comparative government, comparative economic systems, and the like. Similarly, the significant changes that take place in the history of any given society are the changes which occur in its institutional structures. Generally speaking, description and analysis of such change in the past is the province of history as a social science, whereas the study of institutional change in contemporary society is a task for sociology. However, no clear-cut division of labor can be established for history and sociology in this field.

The Structure and the Functions of Social Institutions

A social institution has a structure and a set of functions. The structure consists of the folkways, mores, artifacts, and the patterns of social organization which make it up. The meeting of each of the human needs associated with the basic problem the social institution solves is one of its functions.

To cite the example used earlier in this chapter, the structure of one social institution—the economic system—consists of all the tools, products, skills, techniques, attitudes, values, typical social patterns, and status configurations which we use to solve the problem of getting a living. The meeting of each of the human needs served by these aspects of structure is a function of the economic system. These functions may or may not be generally recognized. Those which are recognized as functions of a given social structure have been called manifest functions as distinct from unrecognized latent functions.[2] For example, recently when a group of married college students were asked why they would like to own a new car, most of them pointed out the utility of a new car in their lives: more dependable transportation, greater safety for wife and kids, more comfort on a long trip, cheaper insurance rates, lower repair bills, and so on. These, then, were for them the manifest functions of new-car ownership. However, although these reasons are probably valid, and although they often express real needs of modern American families, they do not constitute the whole story. Most

---

[1] For a recent discussion of alternative definitions of *institution*, see Ely Chinoy; *Sociological Perspective: Basic Concepts and Their Application* (Studies in Sociology), New York, Random House, Inc., 1954, pp. 16 ff.

[2] Robert K. Merton: *Social Theory and Social Structure*, Glencoe, Ill., The Free Press, 1949, Ch. 1.

of the respondents were not admitting that it is very important for them to appear to be able to afford the newest, most powerful, most chromium-plated automobiles available. A new automobile is a symbol of status, of having enough income over and above that necessary for the provision of the essentials of life to be able to waste some of it on a new and fancy car. And among the derived human needs associated with our competitive economic system is the need of most of us to appear successful. To the extent that this function of new-car ownership is unrecognized by individual Americans who own or who want to own a new car, it is a latent function.

One reason for the latency of some of the functions of our social institutions is that the needs which are being met are not recognized as needs because of a lack of understanding of the nature of man and his society. For instance, some psychologists contend that most people harbor subconscious sexual desires for their parent of the opposite sex, that this desire is sublimated, and that its satisfaction is achieved by means of activities divorced from direct sexual contact with the parent. Now, if all this is true, many people simply do not realize it. Therefore they do not recognize the satisfaction of such desire as a function of any of the activities they engage in.

Another reason for latency concerns the fact that many needs are not considered very honorable and hence most people do not care to admit even to themselves that they respond to them. Most people harbor some hostile and aggressive feelings even toward those whom they regard with great affection. Most of us have felt such feelings, but most of us would prefer not to admit that such feelings account for any specific action we have taken. We would prefer, for example, to feel that we spank our children "for their own good," rather than because the act is a socially acceptable means of expressing our hostility towards them in times of stress.

The reasons for latency are not of primary importance here, however. It is rather the fact of the existence of latent functions that concerns us in this study. This fact is important in that it implies that in our analysis of institutional change we must push beyond the obvious, the admitted and the traditional explanations of human behavior. We must often read between the lines, so to speak, if we are to understand why a given pattern of our culture has developed and why it is changing in the way it is changing.

Since our examples of manifest and latent functions have involved individual, as well as group or societal needs, it is necessary to caution the reader against confusing function with motivation. The two terms are not synonymous. The term *motivation* refers to the reason an individual does something. The term *function* refers to the purpose that a typical behavior pattern serves; and the function of a given pattern of behavior may differ from the motivation for that behavior. For example, one of the functions of marriage is the meeting of the societal need for reproducing the species. On the other hand, the motivations for marriage are many and varied, ranging from fear of the shotgun held by an irate father to the final fulfilment of a deep, undying passion; but it is doubtful that anybody marries in order to reproduce the species. The distinction between motivation and function is an important one and, as Merton points out, the failure to recognize it has led to some remarkably fallacious analyses of society.[3]

Summary

In summary, then, the changes that are important to us are those which affect the efficiency of our culture and social organization of mankind and the meeting of human needs. Human needs may be either basic or derived, universal or particular, societal, group, or individual in nature.

Therefore, in order to study the changes that occur in the way our needs are met, we choose an analytical unit which functions to meet human needs, namely, the social institution. A social institution, as we use the concept, is defined as a group of folkways, mores, and artifacts which together with a pattern of social organization serve the human needs associated with the basic problem of human life.

Any social institution has a structure and a set of functions. The structure of a social institution consists of the folkways, mores, artifacts, and the pattern of social organization which make it up. In terms of function, a social institution exists in order to meet the human needs associated with the basic problem of human life which it solves. These functions may either be manifest or latent. Manifest functions are those which are readily recognized by the individuals of the society as purposes of their institutional structure. Latent functions are those which are not so generally recognized.

---

[3] *Ibid.*, esp. pp. 25–27, 61–64.

chapter two

Why Society Changes

Change in Social Institutions

Since social institutions exist in order to solve the basic problems of human life, and since these basic problems themselves seem to be very slow to change, it might seem at first thought that rapid change in our social institutions is rather unlikely. One might argue that since our basic problems are obviously solved pretty well—after all, if they weren't, we wouldn't be alive today—change in the ways we solve those problems must be slow to occur. As a matter of fact, compared to the speed of change in such areas as fashions, fads, political personnel, and the like, our social institutions are quite stable and are indeed relatively slow to change. Also it is certainly the case that change in our institutional structure is very likely to be vigorously resisted by some elements of our society precisely because such change seems to them to threaten a satisfactory solution to the problems that they face.

However, social institutions must function in order to meet the human needs associated with the basic problems of life. It is to be expected, therefore, that social institutions will change when human needs change. They may also be expected to change when for some reason they fail to meet already existing human needs. And, finally, they may be expected to change when new materials and artifacts suggest better ways to meet old needs, or when the exhaustion of old materials makes it impossible to meet the old needs in the old ways. Let us consider each of these three situations.

1. *Social institutions change when human needs change.*

Change in the basic biological needs of mankind is bound to be slow. Some of the basic human needs are by their very nature unchanging. For instance, as long as human beings are animals, they will need sustenance, they will need to procreate, and they will need to protect themselves from danger. Of course, as environment changes there will be some change in the kinds of dangers facing humanity, but this process is very slow. Presumably some of man's biological needs may change in the course of his evolution as an animal, but this factor could account for little of the social change we observe. Certainly it does not account for the rapid social change experienced by Americans during the last fifty years.

However, it is quite likely that many of the derived needs of humanity do change. Some of them, of course, are quite stable, especially those which we described as universal human needs. But particular needs of individuals and of groups can and do change rapidly. After all, the individuals who make up society are constantly changing through birth, growth, death, and migration, and there must be a resulting variation of their particular needs. Furthermore, our society is not alone in this world and changes in the societies of others may create new needs in ours. The rise of the Soviet Union as a military power is obviously affecting us in this way.

Another reason for change in the needs of our people lies in the fact that institutional changes that have already taken place may create new derived needs. An example is that the change in our mode of transportation from the horse to the automobile obviously has created the need in our society for a high-speed highway system. So needs may change for a number of reasons, and their change contributes to a need for change in our social institutions.

2. *Social institutions change when they fail to meet existing human needs.*

Social institutions sometimes fail to meet needs even when the specific need in question has not changed. In the first place, some human needs are at times more compelling than others and sometimes we sacrifice the meeting of one group of needs in order to meet another. For example, in time of war we circumscribe our own freedom and regiment ourselves in order to effect a concerted effort to defend ourselves and to win the war. In so doing we quite consciously restrict the meeting of many of our individual needs. Our men congregate in such a manner that their desires for sexual gratification, family life, individual expression, and the like cannot possibly be met satisfactorily. They do so in order that they may meet the more important need for protection of themselves and their countrymen.

Thus, in order to serve one function of our institutional structure, we allow it to develop what we may call dysfunctions—failures to meet human needs.[1] This situation not only occurs in time of crisis, but also exists to a lesser extent at all times, for what is functional in terms of one set of needs or one basic problem may be dysfunctional in terms of another set of needs or basic problem. For instance, the competitive nature of our economic system is generally functional for efficient production and distribution, but it may be at the same time dysfunctional in that because of it our psychological need for a feeling of security is often unmet.

A second reason why dysfunctions arise, why needs fail to be met, derives from the fact that some of the functions of our social institutions are latent. When we revise our system of doing things in order to better serve a manifest function, there may result unexpected dysfunctions, because the latent functions of the earlier setup are not being met by the new one. An example commonly accompanies clean-up-the-government drives in some of our municipalities. Periodically in many cities the public becomes aroused over

---

[1] The concepts of function and dysfunction are analyzed by Robert K. Merton in *Social Theory and Social Structure*, Chapter 1. However, their meanings differ somewhat in this context from that of Merton. In his usage functions are "those observed consequences which make for the adaptation or adjustment of a given system" (p. 50), whereas in our usage a function is simply the meeting of a human need. Note, however, that since social integration is here regarded as a societal need, *function* in Merton's sense is included in *function* in our sense. Similarly, where dysfunctions are, for Merton, observed consequences which are socially disintegrative in nature, the term in our sense denotes, simply, a failure to meet a human need.

the fact that its government is dishonest, is supporting criminals, is taking graft, and so on. In the name of honesty and efficiency in government the aroused public "throws the rascals out." Often, to the surprise of observers, this has resulted in the growth of brand new corruption, has materially weakened community spirit and caused great dissatisfaction with the governmental system itself. One reason for this lies in the fact that many of the functions of some crooked political machines are latent—not recognized—and hence ignored. The purpose of the reform movements has been to effect the manifest functions of efficient, economical government. When such is achieved, however, we have too often been left dissatisfied because some needs we did not recognize have gone unmet.

It was the finding of Lincoln Steffens, the famous muckraker, for instance, that the honest governments in the city of New York were unable to recover as much stolen property for prominent people as were the dishonest governments. The reasons seemed to be that the dishonest governments, dealing with criminals regularly, knew who they were, and when the complaint of the citizen was strong enough and the citizen was important enough, the corrupt police authorities knew who had done the stealing and could make arrangements for the goods to be returned for a small settlement. Thus, insurance claims and rates were lower under the dishonest government than under the honest one! Similarly, citizens of a city where there is a completely impartial and honest police force are very likely to express dissatisfaction when they are unable to fix fines for speeding, or when members of prominent families get arrested for drunkenness.

So another reason that social institutions fail to meet existing needs is related to the fact that previous social changes may have failed to set up patterns which would fulfill latent functions. When in the course of events those needs which therefore go unmet become important enough, it is likely that the social institutions involved will change to meet them.

3. *Social institutions change when new materials suggest better ways of meeting needs or when exhaustion of old materials makes it impossible to meet the needs in the old ways.*

The invention of the atomic bomb has obviously necessitated changes in the role government must play and in the way our military power is organized. Similarly, the discovery of oil and natural gas as efficient fuel has wrought great changes in the coal industry, allowed the development of the internal combustion engine which in turn allowed the development of the automobile, truck, bus, and so on. It is clear that automotive transportation has in turn changed family activities considerably, and has made people increasingly dependent upon large centers of trade and commerce and much less dependent upon services which are available in small communities. There are many other cases in which the development of technological materials, new raw materials, and the threat of losing old ones has created new needs which in turn necessitate change in social institutions.

The Institutional Structure of Society as a Dynamic Equilibrium

The foregoing discussion has implied one basic and very important fact about social institutions: they are interconnected and mutually dependent.

After all, each of us as individuals is affected by most of the social institutions of our society. The folkways and mores are not only the normal ways of doing, thinking, and feeling; they are also, for the most part, our personal ways, and they must make a consistent pattern if we are to maintain sanity. If, for instance, our attitudes and values and behavior in our roles as family members were in complete opposition to the way we think, feel, and act as citizens of our country participating in its government, we simply would not be able to make sense out of our lives, and the result would be considerable psychological torment. Therefore, if social institutions did not fit together at least enough to make somewhat of a total sense, we as individuals simply would not be able to adjust to them; we would be highly motivated to change them so that they did fit together, at least reasonably well.

However, the total sense of our institutional structure is never quite perfect. Social institutions do not fit together with the perfection of a jigsaw puzzle. To some extent they often contradict one another. This is partly due to the nature and the multiplicity of the human needs which they serve. Many human needs contradict one another. Societal needs may be counter to the needs of individuals and groups within the societies. The particular needs of specific individuals and groups may be in direct opposition to the particular needs of other individuals and groups. Man's culture and social organization therefore are in a constant state of flux as both major and minor adjustments are made in order to meet the various needs as they rise and decline in importance.

Thus, social institutions must often adjust in terms of one another. The competitive nature of our economic system, for instance, guarantees the "failure" of some individuals and groups. After all, competition implies, as does a race, that not everyone wins, and although competition functions to make for greater efficiency of our systems of production and distribution, it also has the dysfunction of failing to meet adequately the needs of those individuals and groups who are among the economic losers. This fact makes it necessary that another social institution, the government, adjust itself so that the dysfunctions of the economic system can be compensated for. In response to this need government has set up programs of unemployment insurance, social security, and relief. These programs in turn necessitate the readjustment of the economic system, because they have in part pulled the teeth of the threat of failure as a motivation for some people to produce efficiently. A new set of problems has arisen, new adjustments will have to be made which in turn will create new needs, and so ad infinitum.

This pattern of institutional readjustment applies not only to the social institutions of government and the economic system, but to all of the social institutions of our society. All of them are in some measure constantly adjusting so that conflicts within themselves can be modified. Generally speaking, a change in one institution usually gives rise to change in other institutions, since people are motivated to fashion their culture in such a manner that their personal behavior may be consistent and understandable.

In other words, the institutional structure of society can be thought of as a dynamic imperfect equilibrium subject to constant change.

We can think of social change, then, as a process which once begun tends to continue for a very long time, as change in one part of our social structure gives rise to dysfunctions in another, creating the need for further change, and so on. This process, however, is complicated by the fact that some parts of our institutional structure are more resistant to change than are others.

Of course, all social institutions by their very nature are resistant to change. Folkways and mores are grounded in the habits of human beings and (as anyone who has tried to give up smoking knows) human beings find it difficult to change their habits. Not only that, but most of us have based our lives and made our plans with the supposition that our social organization and our manners of doing things are going to remain essentially stable. We resist as a matter of self-interest many changes suggested to us. We are often afraid that basic revisions in our society and in our culture will leave us stranded among our old, useless plans and preparations.

We have become aware, however, that the economy of our country is based upon the development of new products and the distribution of new machines and we have come to expect such developments. We are no longer inclined to scoff at the wildest fantasy of the technological dreamers because we have seen so many of these fantasies come true and have successfully adjusted to the use of so many new machines. On the other hand, there are some things which we hold sacred—our religion, some of the fundamental tenets of our Bill of Rights, our belief in progress, our ideas of good and bad. And these aspects of our culture tend to change much more slowly than our technology, our artifacts, and our skills. William F. Ogburn has labeled this situation a "cultural lag."[2]

Social change, then, is a process which once begun, tends to continue for a very long time, but which is more likely to begin in those areas of our institutional structure which are most secular. The process of change is likely to be least rapid and most convulsive in those areas which we hold most sacred.

The Overwhelming Event as the Agent of Change

Even those most secular areas of our institutional structure are somewhat resistant to change. Any change in institutional structure means that some vested interests are threatened and that old habits must be broken and new ones established. Therefore it seems reasonable to suppose that the beginning impetus for a wave of social change must be strong enough to demand the readjustment of established habits and attitudes. It must be some overwhelming occurrence which affects the human needs which our institutions meet.

Abbott P. Herman has suggested the concept *agent of change* to designate those seminal changes which require the readjustment of the rest of our institutional structure. He writes:

An instrument of change is an agent (or agency) like a mechanical invention, a population trend, a natural cataclysm (flood or earthquake). Most instruments are caused by man's ways. The causes of a few—tornadoes and earthquakes, for

[2] William F. Ogburn: *Social Change*, New York, The Viking Press, Inc., 1950.

example—probably have little connection with man's activities. All agents have this in common: they act as spearheads of change, as the battering-rams of the social process. From them stem most of the problem effects. Without them no serious disturbances would arise.

Does this mean that such instruments are a first cause of social change? It does not. Agents of change arise out of the interminable and gradually developing process. . . . They emerge when many antecedent variables converge in a locale to form something new, something with the potentiality for great and far-reaching effects.

In this sense an agent of change may be said to be, if not a first cause, then a cause of prime importance . . .[3]

In other words, Herman suggests that there are overwhelming events which take place to which society must adjust and that these events are seminal to the resulting process of interinstitutional readjustment which constitutes a wave of social change. He classifies these agents of change into five categories: mechanical inventions, population movements, natural resources, natural occurrences, and physiological changes. Of these, he rightfully emphasizes mechanical inventions as by far the most important in contemporary American culture, for major mechanical inventions affect our way of life to the core. There can be no question that our society has changed in response to the development of radio, television, the motion picture, the automobile, weapons of mass destruction, and the x-ray, to name but a few examples.

The institutional structures dealing with the advance of technology are among those structures most prone to change because such change nets profits, makes life easier, and hence finds ready acceptance. Furthermore, mechanical inventions tend to accumulate as more and more are made. Their effects on society also tend to accumulate. For instance, the invention of the use of steam as a force for running an engine gave rise to untold numbers of other inventions which have forced changes in American life. The steam engine used in locomotion on land and on sea was a prime factor in the development of the cattle industry in the West, which in turn supplied an important economic basis for the growth of the cities of the Middle West. The steam engine enabled our huge nation to tie itself together into a single economic unit. Similarly, the use of steam power in driving industrial machines made possible the development of mass-production techniques which in turn made for the death of many old skills and the development of many new ones. It was also a major factor in America's change from a rural agricultural society to an urban industrial one.

In his study of the problem involvements of mechanical inventions Louis M. Hacker writes:

As we have seen, by 1900 the machine had become an important factor in American life. But in the three decades following, the machine was to become mightier and have a more pervasive influence—it was to produce more, furnish more comforts, conquer new domains, until by 1930, Americans began to regard it very much as the hallmark, the peculiar, distinguishing sign, of our whole

[3] Abbott P. Herman: *An Approach to Social Problems*, Boston, Ginn & Company, 1949, pp. 54–55. Used by permission.

civilization. The machine was ruthless: it broke down privacy, swept away ancient trades, destroyed skill, created technological unemployment, wasted natural resources, standardized and sometimes vulgarized taste, quickened the tempo of men's lives and brought in a crop of new psychoneurotic disorders, made warfare a horror and an inferno, constricted the size of the world until men almost everywhere were performing their daily tasks in the same way, employing their idle moments in much the same fashion, and very largely thinking the same thoughts. Yet the machine was beneficent, too: it was releasing mankind from the bitter, backbreaking labor of centuries and was making life comfortable for the toiling masses; it was producing, if only slowly, more leisure time; it was turning out more goods. True, great inequalities in wealth and income still existed; and periodic breakdowns, or business crises, continued to occur, during which production slowed down and large numbers of persons were thrown out of work to suffer privations and often real want. The fault, however, lay not in the machine but in the nature of its ownership and the uses to which it was put by business.

The machine, too, made for more color and variety in our daily lives; it put amusements within the reach of all; it dressed the humblest shopgirl in clothes whose designs, at least, were the work of the smartest Paris salons. It was making life healthier and more secure against the ravages of nature; it was making men bolder and more certain of themselves; if it was destroying old crafts— glass blowers, weavers, cabinetmakers—it was creating new groups of artisans— radio mechanics, sanitary engineers, chauffeurs, steel construction workers. Thus the machine worked for both good and ill, and toward which side the balances tipped only a rash or a prophetic person might venture to say.[4]

Mechanical inventions being accumulative, being readily accepted by a nation interested in making profits, by a people interested in living ever more comfortably, having plenty of capital to invest and a great propensity to consume are undoubtedly primary agents of change in American society.

Herman's second category of agents of change is population movements. This is to some extent a misnomer, for the concept includes not only migratory movements of population across the face of the earth, but also other changes in population such as growth and decline in size, changes in population composition, age trends, and the like. Migratory movements are perhaps the most dramatic of these in their effect upon the institutional structure of society. Most Americans can recall the tremendous stresses and strains which resulted from the movement of our population during World War II into the areas where our defense production expanded the employment opportunities enormously. We recall the race riots in Detroit and other cities which resulted from the sudden influx of rural Southerners, both Negro and white, into a situation where the patterns of segregation were new to them. Many of us are living today in the jerrybuilt houses which were thrown together in order to accommodate the thousands of newcomers into our industrial areas, and it is clear that such migrations can set violent change in motion.

The fact that our population is growing older is also requiring us to adjust our institutional structure to meet the needs of the expanding group of aged people among us. The effect of immigrants from foreign lands upon

[4] Louis M. Hacker: *American Problems of Today*, New York, F. S. Crofts & Company, 1938, pp. 71–72. Used by permission of Appleton-Century-Crofts, Inc.

our social structure is recalled whenever we hear America referred to as "the great melting pot," and we realize that our rapidly expanding population during the years of our growth as a nation was a major factor in our ability to develop the powerful economy that we have. It is clear that changes in population require changes in our social structure and therefore they constitute an important type of agent of social change.

Changes in natural resources, that is, increases and decreases in the supply of various exploitable raw materials, constitute the third category of agents of social change, according to Herman. This kind of change occurs in several ways. In the first place, old raw materials become depleted as are, for example, the high-grade iron ore deposits in America today. In the second place, new sources of power are developed so that previously unused raw materials can be utilized. The growth of the importance of radioactive materials to provide atomic energy is an example of this. In the third place, new sources of old resources are discovered and developed, as is the case when a new oil field is found.

Any of these situations may certainly set social change in motion, for they all require almost immediate adjustment of our economic system which in turn calls forth adjustments in other areas of our institutional structure.

The last two of Herman's categories of agents of change—natural occurrences and physiological changes—are not as likely to be brought about through the activities of man, but rather are usually factors of his natural environment. They probably have less effect on modern society than do the first three of the categories of agents of change, all of which result from the activities of human beings. Natural occurrences, such as floods, tornadoes, earthquakes, insect pests, and the like, certainly have made social adjustments necessary; but for the most part as society grows more and more urbanized, it becomes less and less directly dependent upon the exigencies of nature. However, when metropolitan governments are reorganized in order to cope with the threat of water shortages or paralyzing blizzards and when agencies such as the Tennessee Valley Authority are created in order to control floods and to utilize water power, whole series of changes are likely to be set in motion. Therefore, natural occurrences and the steps we take to control them certainly can be important agents of social change.

Physiological changes such as disease and other organic pathologies have at times caused people to change their way of living. The Black Death in England during the Renaissance had an unquestioned effect upon the nature of British society. Similarly, the influenza epidemics, the rise of cancer and infantile paralysis in American society have called forth the development of new organizations and methods to deal with these diseases, and in so doing may have set in motion institutional adjustments which are far reaching in their effects. Both natural occurrences and physiological changes can be agents of social change, but it is doubtful that in modern American society they are as important as mechanical inventions, population movements, and changes in natural resources.

Each of Herman's five categories of agents of change are internal to a given society; they do not include those overwhelming events or occurrences which result from the actions of societies other than ours and from international actions. Wars and the threat of wars, economic competition among nations, economic and political domination, the changes in the balance of power in world affairs, and world-wide economic crises such as the great depression of the 1930s cannot be attributed to events within one society alone. Obviously it takes at least two nations to make a war and although the actions of one society may influence changes in the balance of power, such change must also be contributed to by others. The economic crises which are worldwide in scope can certainly not be explained in terms of American society alone. We are, in fact, only a portion, and a very small portion, of the society of the world. What happens to the people of the rest of that world affects us, and often the behavior of another society constitutes an event overwhelming enough to require large-scale adjustment on our part. Our society has changed considerably in response to World War II, the Korean conflict, and the cold war with the USSR. Americans today hold values and do things because of these events which they would never have thought of doing twenty years ago. For example, the military as an important factor of American society in peacetime is new to Americans. Prior to World War II, a substantial portion of our citizenry felt that European wars had nothing to do with us and that we had no responsibility to the rest of the world. Even those who still feel that America should not concern itself with the fate of other people feel constrained to state their point of view in very different terms from those used prior to 1941. Americans have come to accept as a matter of course that a major portion of the national budget will be spent on national defense and the military career is increasingly looked upon as an honorable and necessary one.

The depression of the 1930s also left American society its legacy of important change. How foreign to the American nature of the twenties seemed such measures as social security programs and federal government relief! Today we take such programs as a matter of course and recognize them as an important function of our government. All in all, the effects of neighboring societies upon us constitute a very important category of agents of social change.

Summary

The process of social change can be described as a series of waves of change, each wave beginning with some overwhelming event or series of events which strikes at the function of one or more of our social institutions necessitating changes in its structure. We have noted six types of such agents of change: mechanical inventions, population change, changes in natural resources, natural occurrences, physiological changes, and the effects of neighboring societies upon ours. These agents of change usually affect those areas of our institutional structure which are most prone to change, that is, the portions which we hold least sacred. As the structural changes necessitated by the agent of change are made in the affected institutions, dysfunctions may arise for other parts of our institutional structure, thus necessitating new changes of structure, and so on as our whole institutional structure makes the adjustments necessary to maintain some degree of equilibrium.

chapter three

How Social Change Takes Place

It must be remembered, of course, that social institutions are not capable of changing themselves. A social institution is, after all, an abstraction, conceived by social scientists in order to help them understand the nature of culture and of social organization. It is not an entity which can think and act for itself. Only human beings can do that, and hence social change can only come about through the interaction of people. Therefore, in order to understand social change, how social institutions become modified, it is necessary to review our understanding of the mechanisms of human interaction.

When two or more people communicate and modify one another's behavior, social interaction is taking place. This concept covers a wide range of human activity, and incidentally the totality of the field of sociology. Social interaction is taking place between a couple when they say good night in front of the dormitory. Interaction is also taking place between you and me as you read this. In fact, you and Shakespeare interact when you read *Hamlet* if the reading of *Hamlet* modifies your behavior (that is, puts you to sleep, excites you, or interests you). It is of course doubtful that you will modify Shakespeare's behavior.

Social Process in Social Change

Since the concept of social interaction does cover such a wide territory, it is useful for the purpose of analysis to develop general types of social interaction. These types are often classified as social processes. Social processes, as kinds of social interaction, may be divided into two main types: those which operate to enable men to get along harmoniously within the existing institutional framework and those which allow men to oppose one another either within or without the existing institutional framework. Wilson and Kolb call the former *conjunctive* and the latter *disjunctive* social processes.[1]

Among the most important of the conjunctive social processes is cooperation. *Cooperation* is that kind of human interaction in which men get together to accomplish a common purpose. When a contractor hires carpenters, plumbers, foremen, brickmasons, hod carriers, and so on to build a house, these men come together and work together for the purpose of

---

[1] Logan Wilson, and William L. Kolb: *Sociological Analysis*, New York, Harcourt, Brace & Co., 1949, pp. 681–682.

completing the building. They are engaging in cooperative human interaction. As far as social change is concerned, when people organize in order
to create an invention and later to produce and market it, they are cooperat-
ing in a manner which may well result in widespread social change. Similarly when the institutional structure develops dysfunctions, so that sufficiently important human needs go unmet and people become dissatisfied
with their lot, men may band together to do something about it. In such
a case, human cooperation is directed specifically at changing the conditions
of life, and hence as a social process it is a most important mechanism of
social change.

Another important conjunctive social process is _accommodation,_ which
is the type of interaction whereby two individuals or groups adjust their
behavior in order to get along with one another. A man and a woman who
marry must accommodate themselves in some measure to the needs and
the desires of one another, or else the relationship is likely to be short lived.
Accommodation may bring about social change as when the dominant
element of a society receives a number of immigrants into its midst and
modifies its own behavior in order to keep intergroup tension and hostility
at a minimum. That is, the members of the dominant element adjust their
lives in order to include the new group, and the members of the new group
in turn change their manner of living and thinking so that they are acceptable to the dominant element. The behavioral and attitudinal changes that
result from this process often constitute important social and cultural
change.

Associated with the kind of accommodation that goes on between an
immigrant group and a dominant group is _assimilation._ This is the process
whereby two groups having disparate cultures fuse into a single group with
a common culture. For instance, many immigrant groups, after a long-term
process of accommodation often lasting several generations, become fused
into an almost imperceptible element of the dominant society. During this
process, not only has the immigrant group lost its identity as a separate
group, but the dominant culture has been altered to some extent by including within its institutional structure elements of the foreign culture intro-
duced by the immigrants.

Two of the most important disjunctive social processes are competition
and conflict. *Competition* is that type of human interaction whereby two
or more individuals or groups attempt to attain the same goal to the exclu-
sion of the others attempting to attain it, as, for instance, when two young
men are courting the same girl. In competing people operate within the
institutional structure, that is, they conform to the folkways and mores of
their community. They are also usually more interested in obtaining the
goal than in hurting one another.

Conflict on the other hand occurs when two or more individuals or
groups are primarily interested in hurting one another, rather than obtaining a goal. Thus, if the young lady mentioned above somehow gets her
signals crossed and schedules a date with each of her swains at the same
time, she may witness a conflict on her front porch. Both young men may
forget the purpose of their call and concentrate upon the alteration of one
another's features. In such a case they are no longer operating within the

folkways and mores of the community; they are simply in a fight.* No longer are they competing; they are in conflict.

Both competition and conflict as social processes may be important mechanisms of social change. As groups and individuals compete for various goals they may produce new and better ways of doing things, new and better products, and so on, which may in turn cause very basic changes. Furthermore, as political groups, for example, compete with one another for office, they may, in their attempt to win votes, suggest and carry through policy changes which are designed to better meet some human needs and which may constitute important social changes.

Similarly, conflict may result in social change. Indeed, Marxian thinkers among others, interpret all social change in terms of conflict. They believe that there is a constant struggle between economic classes for dominance and for control of the tools of production. According to Marxian theorists, in modern, capitalistic society this conflict takes place between the bourgeoisie, the class which at present controls the tools of production through its ownership of money, and the proletariat, the class which in their view actually adds the value to products through the skill and the toil it contributes. Marxists see political, economic, and social reforms as bones tossed by the bourgeois masters to their proletarian "dogs" in order to still the voice of their rebellion, and they look for basic social change to take place only when the proletariat rises as a class and takes over control of the tools of production from the bourgeoisie. Marxists often argue that such a revolution is inevitable, for the dependency of the bourgeoisie upon its labor force is actual, whereas the dependency of the proletariat upon its bosses is only illusory. Therefore, they feel, as soon as the reformist's "bones" give the proletarians enough power and as soon as these "underdogs" recognize that as a class they have common interests, they will realize that there is no need to continue in exploitative slavery, and hence they, by virtue of their superior numbers and their essential role in economic life, will decide to put an end to it.

While the existence in the United States of a class struggle in the Marxian sense is highly questionable, the Marxists' reasoning does point out that conflict and the threat of conflict can be mechanisms of widespread social change, especially when the "powers that be" accommodate themselves to new situations by instituting reforms in order to forestall threatened strife.

Sociocultural Drift

The nature of social change varies with the type of the social interaction that brings about the change. Sometimes the interaction is specifically directed to causing or resisting a given social change. Men organize, cooperate, accommodate, assimilate, compete, and sometimes enter into conflict over a specific social issue or set of issues. Their interaction is oriented toward a proposed social change. On the other hand, much social change results from human interaction which is directed toward ends other than

---

* The editor is disinclined to suggest qualification of this homely passage. But he must note that such fights are usually also structured by cultural conventions.—C. H. P.

change itself. The latter type of social change can be called *sociocultural drift*.

For instance, there is quite a bit of evidence that during the past fifty years the courtship practices of American youth have altered considerably. Kinsey found that although it is likely that young people have always engaged in considerable sex play during courtship, both the incidence and the variety of premarital petting reported by American women has increased considerably during the last half century.[2] It is also probable that the frequency of casual dancing, and the frankness of conversations concerning sex between young men and women has increased during the same period. Unchaperoned dates are certainly much more common now than they were at the beginning of this century. These changes have taken place relatively gradually. They were not the result of revolutionary efforts on the part of interested individuals, and while occasionally someone decries the "moral laxity of our youth," these changes have not given rise to any concerted opposition. Rather, young people have gone about the pleasant business of courtship making up their minds as they went along as to what behavior was acceptable in the situations in which they found themselves. As the availability of the family automobile gave them mobility and a certain degree of anonymity; as the changing mores of the society as a whole have allowed them to observe various forms of lovemaking more or less expertly portrayed on the movie screen; as they have experienced more and better sex education both at school and at home, their definition of socially acceptable behavior and their expectations of one another's responses have undergone considerable change.

Similarly, changes in laws, in administrative patterns in business practices, and in most other areas of our life take place in just such an unplanned and unheralded manner. As people learn more, experiment, work out problems concerning their daily life, and as they communicate their ideas and methods to one another, major social changes take place with none of the reformer's zeal or the revolutionist's violence. It is probable that such sociocultural drift accounts for much of the social change that occurs in America today and perhaps this form of change is the most important, if not the most dramatic, form that exists.

Social Movements

The process of change that most frequently makes the newspaper headlines for its drama is that in which the human interaction involved is specifically directed toward the accomplishment of change. Organized efforts to effect social change are called *social movements*. Blumer writes:

Social movements can be viewed as collective enterprises to establish a new order of life. They have their inception in a condition of unrest, and derive their motive power on one hand from dissatisfaction with the current form of life, and on the other hand from wishes and hopes for a new scheme or system of living. The career of a social movement depicts the emergence of a new order of life. In its beginning, a social movement is amorphous, poorly organized, and without form; the collective behavior is on the primitive level . . . , and the

[2] Kinsey, Pomeroy, Martin, Gebhard, *et al.*: *Sexual Behavior in the Human Female*, Philadelphia, W. B. Saunders Co., 1953, p. 268.

mechanisms of interaction are the elementary, spontaneous . . . As a social movement develops, it takes on the character of a society. It acquires organization and form, a body of customs and traditions, established leadership, and enduring division of labor, social rules, and social values—in short, a culture, a social organization, and a new scheme of life.[3]

Blumer states that specific movements (as opposed to general social movements, which we would include as a type of sociocultural drift) may primarily be classified as either reformative or revolutionary in nature. These two types, according to Blumer, differ in the scope of their objectives, the vantage points of their attacks, their degree of respectability, and their general procedures and tactics. He thinks of the revolutionary movement as seeking to reconstruct the entire social order, as challenging the existing folkways and mores, as refusing the respect of the public at large, as using violence and religious zeal, and as playing upon the frustrations and aggressions of the underprivileged classes of society. The reform movement, on the other hand, is seen by Blumer as seeking to change some specific aspect of the institutional structure, as utilizing the existing code of ethics, as enlisting the respect of the public, and as attempting to influence the politically important elements of the population by an appeal to their self-interest, their values, and their sympathies.[4]

However, Blumer's distinction seems to be somewhat oversimplified. It is, for instance, difficult to conceive of people brought up in a given society challenging all of the existing folkways and mores, or trying to remake the entire social order. Furthermore, there have been social movements which have represented classes other than the most underprivileged of society. The Nazi movement in Germany was indubitably a revolutionary movement; yet it appealed primarily to the middle classes and was financed by major industrialists—hardly underprivileged groups![5]

Actually there is no clear borderline between the two types, their difference being a matter of degree. But one important difference is in the claims of the leaders as to the scope of the objectives of the movement. The New Deal in the American politics of the early 1930s is an example of a large-scale reform movement. Its leaders claimed to be interested in meeting the crisis of the depression, and in structuring the government and its fiscal policy in such a manner that subsequent depressions would be less violent and less hurtful. On the other hand, the Communist Party of the 1920s and early 1930s, an example of a revolutionary movement, claimed as its aim the abolition of the capitalistic system, and the formation of a worldwide, stateless, classless society in which depressions, inflations, and struggles between classes would be unknown. Another major difference between reform and revolutionary movements in general, and these two examples in particular, lies in the nature of the public reaction to them. The New Deal

---

[3] Herbert Blumer: "Collective Behavior," Part IV of *New Outline of the Principles of Sociology.* Ed. Alfred McClung Lee. New York, Barnes & Noble, Inc., 1946, p. 199. Used by permission.

[4] *Ibid.,* pp. 211–214.

[5] Hadley Cantril: *The Psychology of Social Movements,* New York, John Wiley & Sons, Inc., 1941, pp. 246–249.

was very quickly recognized as a legitimate political point of view by the majority of our people, whereas the Communist Party has always been regarded by most with extreme suspicion, distrust, and with the feeling that it is out to wreck the American way of life. The fact that the New Deal resulted in much more permanent and important changes in the American social structure than did the Communist Party does not alter the fact that the New Deal can be considered a reform movement and the Communist Party a revolutionary movement.

It is important to point out, however, that a social movement does not need to be successful according to its own lights in order to effect change. Much of the social welfare program enacted under Bismarck's regime in Germany was set up specifically to lessen the threat to his government by the growing power of the socialist parties, and as a political maneuver succeeded in defeating them. In the United States the Populist Party of the 1890s failed politically, but many of the planks of its platform were adopted by the major parties and enacted into law. And during the first three decades of this century the Industrial Workers of the World, America's most vigorous revolutionary labor union, fell far short of growing into the "One Big Union of All the Workers of the World" that it wished to become, but through its efforts the lumber camps of the Far West and the textile plants of New England became much more pleasant places to work. So social movements may contribute to social change even when they fail to achieve the goals they set up for themselves.

Typical Social Roles in Social Change

Social change is carried on through human interaction, and human beings have statuses and roles to play. When their interaction is specifically directed to a proposed social change, as is the case in social movements, the roles they play and the way they play them directly affect the course of events which results. It is therefore germane to this study to typify some of the most important statuses concerned with social change, and to generalize about the way individuals occupying them play their roles.

Three types of status are of particular interest to us: the leadership, the intelligentsia, and the following. Each of these types of status may be found among organized groups that propose a given social change, organized groups that oppose a given social change, and among those who take no active stand either pro or con, but will be affected by any social change. The roles played by the occupants of each of the three statuses differ to some extent, depending in part upon their position regarding the proposed change.

The Leadership

Any organization of human beings, whether formal or informal, requires leadership in order that its efforts may be directed in a coordinated manner. However, very simple folk societies require formal leadership less than do more complex urban societies. This is because folk societies have a body of long-standing tradition and are extremely slow to change. People engaged in everyday activities within such societies need little personal direction because they play their roles in a way dictated by their traditions; their need for leadership arises primarily in crisis situations in which the established modes of behavior are no longer adequate to meet their needs. This is not to say that folk societies have no formal leadership whatever, just that such leadership is less important in them than it is in more complex societies. In America, where change is rapid, where relationships are more formal, and where many areas of life are not governed by tradition, formal leadership plays a very important role. A joke among Europeans, many of whom live in societies more traditionally oriented than the United States, is that if three strange Americans parachute from an airplane, they will elect a president, a vice-president, and a secretary-treasurer before they hit the ground.

Psychologically, leaders of a group tend to be those members who are aggressive but whose ideas are essentially the same as those of the rest of the members of the group. Another old joke is that a leader is a man who observes the way the crowd is going and who, by means of mighty effort, manages to get one step ahead of it. The implication is that the leader will lose his position if his followers decide to change their course and he fails to change with them. This may be somewhat of an overstatement, but it must at least be noted that most leaders rarely originate points of view or directions of approach; rather they utilize the ideas of others and coordinate their followers in action predicated upon those ideas.

Social scientists have long been interested in the role of leadership in social change. Vilfredo Pareto, an Italian social thinker of great note (1848–1923), felt that social change was linked with the cyclically changing nature of the leadership of society. He felt that people in general could be divided into those whose sentiments led them to orient their actions toward ideal goals and ends, on the one hand, and those whose sentiments led them to an orientation to the immediate opportunities of life, on the other. Associated with each of these personality types are typical kinds of leaders. "Lions" are leaders who believe absolutely in the righteousness of their goals and ideals and who, because of their intense belief, feel justified in gaining and maintaining dominant positions through the use of force. "Foxes," on the other hand, are opportunistic leaders who gain and maintain dominant positions through the use of ruses, deceptions, and the like.

According to Pareto, the two types of leaders tend to alternate in their reigns because each method of ruling has fundamental weaknesses. Force, after all, is expensive and is not conducive to security in office because of the ever-present threat of rebellion. Therefore, the lions, when they are dominant, tend to rely more and more on underlings who are essentially foxes, that is, who are skilled in deception as a technique of maintaining power. The foxes, then, given the opportunity by the lions, make their way to power and maintain themselves there until their lack of long-term objectives makes them vulnerable to a *coup d'état* on the part of the lions. This is known as the *theory of the circulation of elites*, and Pareto felt that the alternating leadership is accompanied by cyclical change in the intellectual and economic aspects of society. Associated with the rule of the lions is deep-seated intellectual faith in the ultimate values of the culture and the economic dominance of the *rentiers*, the timid and unenterprising amassers of fluid capital. On the other hand, the dominance of the foxes is accompanied by predominant skepticism on the intellectual front and the economic leadership of the "speculators," who are daring, but who tend to extravagance and instability.

Pareto's concept of the role of leadership in social change seems somewhat oversimplified, particularly as there seems to be no place in his theory for the effects on society of unsuccessful efforts to gain power. So instead we shall make use of some of the implications of Max Weber's analysis of leadership.

Weber, a German sociologist (1864–1920), discussed leadership in terms of ideal typical constructs. That is, he developed imaginary types which epitomized traits observed in actual leaders. He delineated three such types of leadership: traditional, legal, and charismatic.

The *traditional leader* is one who maintains his leadership because of the long-standing traditions of the community. Weber characterizes the authority of the traditional leader as "the authority of the 'eternal yesterday,' i.e. of the mores sanctified through the unimaginably ancient recognition and habitual orientation to conform. This is 'traditional' domination exercised by the patriarch and the patrimonial prince of yore."[6]

The *legal leader* is one who exercises his authority by virtue of what Weber calls the belief in the validity of legal statute and functional "competence" based on rationally created rules. In this case, obedience is expected in discharging statutory obligations. This is domination as exercised by the modern "servant of the state" and by all those bearers of power who in this respect resemble him."[7]

Finally, the *charismatic leader* is, according to Weber, one who commands the personal devotion of his followers because of the qualities of his personality. In particular, he has the quality which Weber calls *charisma*. Weber writes:

There is the authority of the extraordinary and personal *gift of grace* (charisma), the absolutely personal devotion and personal confidence in revelation, heroism, or other qualities of individual leadership. This is "charismatic" domination, as exercised by the prophet or—in the field of politics—by the elected war lord, the plebiscitarian ruler, the great demagogue, or the political party leader.[8]

For the purposes of our analysis we will combine the first two of Weber's concepts and classify both traditional and legal leaders as legitimate in contrast to charismatic leaders. These classifications are ideal typical constructs; actual leaders are neither purely legitimate nor purely charismatic. Even the most fiery demagogue is likely to have some legal status, and even the dullest elected official is likely to have some personal following. The classification is useful, however, in that it can be shown that some people

---

[6] Max Weber: "Politics as a Vocation," Chapter IV of *From Max Weber: Essays in Sociology.* Translated and edited by H. H. Gerth and C. Wright Mills. New York, Oxford University Press, Inc., 1946, pp. 78–79.

[7] *Ibid.*, p. 79.

[8] *Ibid.*, p. 79. Used by permission. Copyright 1946 by Oxford University Press, Inc.

exercise primarily charismatic authority while others exercise primarily legitimate authority.

As Blumer noted, social movements arise out of a condition of unrest. It is possible to develop an organization dedicated to social change only when there is a substantial number of people who are dissatisfied with life as it is currently being lived. At such times people are eager for a leadership which can with authority promise them salvation from the evils which they feel that they endure. Charisma can best supply such authority. Legitimate leadership usually does not suffice, for the legitimate leadership was in power when the dysfunctions giving rise to the dissatisfaction developed. In periods of social unrest some of the institutional patterns of contemporary society are being questioned, and leadership which bases its authority upon current mores is also likely to be questioned. Organizations proposing social change are therefore likely to be led by charismatic leaders, particularly when the changes they are advocating strike deeply into the institutional structure.

Generally speaking, when organizations attack the status quo and suggest change, they are met with organized opposition. The very existence of proposals for change constitute a threat in and of themselves to those who have a vested interest in life as it is currently being lived. Consequently, there often arises at such periods countermovements, sometimes using tactics similar to the movements they oppose; frequently, although not always, the leadership of such countermovements is also charismatic in nature.

The existence of charismatic leadership is in itself a threat to the legitimate leadership of the society, because the charismatic leader commands a following which is much more vigorous and devoted than the following of the legitimate leader. Consequently, legitimate leaders often find themselves in the middle, so to speak, opposed not only to the movement proposing change, but to its opposition as well.

The Intelligentsia

The intelligentsia may be regarded as consisting of those who are professionally concerned with the development and expression of ideas. Among the intelligentsia are many editors, authors, poets, musicians, artists, speechwriters, teachers, and lecturers. As far as organized effort to propose or oppose social change is concerned, they occupy themselves with the development and dissemination of ideologies. In other words, they conceive the directions of social movements; they develop the arguments supporting the claims of each side of any issue; and they build and support the system of ideas and values by which people live, and in terms of which people make the decisions which determine the course of history. Intellectuals can be characterized according to the type of thought with which they deal. Karl Mannheim has delineated two contrasting modes of thought: ideologic and utopian.[9]

Ideologic thought is that kind of thinking which is essentially defensive of the status quo. The ideas expressed by ideologic thinkers are those which

---

[9] Karl Mannheim: *Ideology and Utopia: An Introduction to the Sociology of Knowledge*, New York, Harcourt, Brace & Co., 1936.

tend to reinforce mores and values which are currently held. Such thought offers an explanation and a justification of life as it is currently being lived, and emphasizes the positive aspects of the things we have and the negative aspects of the consequences of change.

Utopian thought, on the other hand, is essentially critical of the status quo. The ideas expressed by utopian thinkers are those which propose new attitudes and new values. Such thought offers an explanation of existing evils and a justification of a program for change, and emphasizes the negative aspects of the current social scene and the positive aspects of the consequences of change.

It is of interest to note that a single term may be either utopian or ideologic, depending upon how it is used. Contrast, for example, the idea of liberty as used in Patrick Henry's famous address with the same term as used in our pledge of allegiance. When Patrick Henry reached the end of his speech before the Virginia House of Burgesses on the eve of The Revolutionary War, he fervently cried, "Give me liberty or give me death!" He used the concept in a decidedly utopian context. On the other hand, when a school child stands with hand over heart and solemnly declares that the flag to which he declares his allegiance is the flag of a land where there is "liberty and justice for all," he is using the concept in a distinctly ideologic manner.

Ideology and utopia used in this sense are ideal typical constructs. They describe the end points of a continuum of types of thought. Actual thought is probably never completely utopian or completely ideologic, and may in fact be objective, that is, neither utopian nor ideologic. Nevertheless, if an intelligentsia tends to be critical of the status quo and tends to support proposals for change, it can be thought of as primarily utopian; but if it tends to resist change and to justify the status quo, it can be classed as ideological. The intellectual output associated with organized effort to promote social change is, of course, usually utopian.

The ideology of a social movement must accomplish at least three purposes. In the first place, it must provide an explanation of the evils which the discontented people who comprise the following feel they are experiencing. The Industrial Workers of the World, for instance, made use of the Marxian concept of the class struggle in explaining to the social outcasts to whom they wished to appeal their lowly position in life. The preamble to the constitution of the I.W.W. began with the following words: "The working class and the employing have nothing in common. There can be no peace so long as hunger and want are found among millions of working people, and the few who make up the employing class have all the good things of life."

In the second place, the ideology must suggest a solution to the problems confronting the discontented following so that they may feel justified in taking action against the institutional structure that exists. The second clause of the preamble to the constitution of the I.W.W. thus reads, "Between these two classes a struggle must go on until the workers of the world organize as a class, take possession of the earth and the machinery of production and abolish the wage system."

A pamphlet titled *The Revolutionary I.W.W.* by Grover H. Perry was distributed to the rank and file of the movement. It presented a concept of the goals of the movement.

We fold our arms. The mills close. Industry is at a standstill. We then make our proposition to our former masters. It is this: We, the workers have labored long enough to support idlers. From now on, he who does not toil, neither shall he eat. We tear down to build up.

In the place of the present system of society where crime, prostitution and poverty are rampant, a new society will arise. No more prostitutes. Girls will no longer sell their bodies when they can get for themselves the full product of their labor. Crime will disappear as the incentive for it is taken away. Poverty cannot exist where all are workers and none are shirkers. Children instead of working in the mills will be in the schools. Mothers will no longer dread the ordeal of motherhood from [sic] economic reasons. We will grow physically, intellectually and morally. A new race will result, a race that will live for the joy of living, a race that will look with horror upon the pages of history that tell of our present day society.

The Industrial Workers of the World are laying the foundation of a new government. This government will have for its legislative halls the mills, the workshops and factories. Its legislators will be the men in the mills, the workshops and the factories. Its legislative enactments will be those pertaining to the welfare of the workers.

These things are to be. No force can stop them. Armies will be of no avail. Capitalist governments may issue their mandates in vain. The power of the workers—industrially organized—is the only power on earth worth considering. Once they realize that power, classes will disappear, and in their place will be the only useful members of society—the workers.[10]

Finally, the ideology must present suggestions for the tactics of the movement which must follow from the doctrines of the movement. This aspect of the intellectual output usually includes fight songs, parade banners, slogans, and the like. For instance, the I.W.W. songbook contained the following song:

> Tie 'em up! Tie 'em up! that's the
>   way to win.
> Don't notify the bosses 'til the
>   hostilities begin.
> Don't furnish chance for gunmen, scabs,
>   and all their like,
> What you need is the One Big Union and
>   the One Big Strike.

During a strike in 1912 in Lawrence, Massachusetts, the I.W.W.'s strikers carried, among others, a placard reading:

XX century civilization . . . For the progress of the human race we have jails, gallows, guillotines . . . and electric chairs for the people who pay to keep the "Soldiers" to kill them when they revolt against Wood and other czars of capitalism.

[10] Grover H. Perry: *The Revolutionary I.W.W.*, Industrial Workers of the World, Chicago, no date, pp. 11–12.

> Arise!!! Slaves of the world!!!
> No God! No Master!
> One for all and all for one!!![11]

These examples of utopian intellectual output of a revolutionary movement illustrate the way in which established institutional patterns are attacked through the use of symbols and emotion-laden terms to which the following of the movement is likely to react.

The product of the intellectuals who oppose a given social change is, on the other hand, usually ideologic in nature since it consists primarily of an affirmation of the status quo. Such intellectual output will usually attack personally the proponents of social change as well as question the merits of the utopian philosophy itself. For instance, the citizens of Lawrence paraded their righteous indignation at the strike of the I.W.W. as follows:

> For God and Country,
> The Stars and Stripes forever,
> The Red Flag never.
> A Protest against the I.W.W.
> Its principles and methods.[12]

The Following

The nature of the leadership and the intelligentsia of social movements and countermovements have commanded the attention of most social thinkers who have concerned themselves with this type of activity. However, it must not be forgotten that leaders and intellectuals would be powerless without an active and loyal group of followers.

The following of an organization proposing or opposing social change may be regarded as consisting of all the people directly involved who are neither leaders nor members of the intelligentsia. As such, the members of the following exhibit the morale and *esprit de corps* of the organization and are the basic source of its power. The factors that determine whether or not an individual will be sufficiently attracted by a given leadership and body of thought to be motivated to take an active part in an organization supporting them have long been the subject of speculation and study. Marxists attribute willingness to take social action to economic discontent and to class consciousness. Sorel, the philosophical leader of the French Syndicalists, felt that active membership in revolutionary labor organizations was dependent upon the acceptance of the social myth of the general strike and upon the rise of the ethics of warfare among the proletariat. The theories of Marx and Sorel, however, do not explain why some people who are members of the "down-trodden masses" actively resist revolutionary movements and why others are apathetic about them.

Hadley Cantril, an American social psychologist, reminds us that while the attitudes and values of individuals will certainly reflect the mores of the society in which they live, the personalities of individuals vary greatly.

---

[11] Paul F. Brissenden: *The I.W.W., A Study of American Syndicalism*, 2nd ed., New York, Columbia University Press, 1920, p. 19. Used by permission.

[12] *Ibid.* By permission.

After all, the culture itself is not homogeneous, but differs to some degree from group to group, from time to time, and from place to place. Individuals vary in their maturity, in their ability to think critically, in their knowledge, and in their understanding of the nature of causality. Furthermore, individuals differ as to the values and attitudes which they regard as personally significant. Therefore we can expect different men to react differently to the same stimulus even when their social and economic lot is similar.[13] Nevertheless, Cantril believes that it is quite possible to describe the general psychological conditions in which men will act in terms of the suggestions of leaders, agitators, and propagandists even when the action taken is not condoned by the society as a whole. He points out that, generally speaking, human beings organize their experience meaningfully in terms of the mental contexts (frames of reference, attitudes, values) that they have developed during their lives. Thus, for instance, most Americans perhaps could turn on a radio, hear the announcer say, "Preacher Roe is in trouble now, fans. The winning run is on base, there are two out in the last of the ninth, and he's down to the payoff pitch with Stan the Man himself at the plate," and understand the situation perfectly. Most American men would know which teams were playing what game, and regardless of whether the Dodgers or the Cardinals were the team of their preference they would become quite excited. Few would switch to another station just then.

Yet occasionally people find themselves faced with no clear interpretation of a situation or problem perhaps because the standards and frames of reference they utilize do not provide immediate understanding. For example, few Britishers would understand the situation described by the sportscaster above. Of course, most Britishers would not be overly concerned with their lack of understanding; but under certain circumstances, such inability to interpret gives rise to dissatisfactions and tensions. In other words, a desire for meaning is aroused which cannot be satisfied until some acceptable interpretation is found by the individuals thus affected. Three such types of circumstances are important to note in the present context.

First, the desire for meaning may be aroused when a basic individual need goes unmet and no adequate response presents itself to the individual in his desire for satisfaction. Thus, a man out of a job and broke and prevented by the laws and mores of his society from stealing may well be quite frantic in his search for an interpretation of the situation which will enable him to take action to obtain the things he needs. Second, unsatisfied derived individual needs may also give rise to a desire for meaning. For instance, the employee who fails in his efforts to obtain occupational advancement is likely to seek an interpretation of the situation which defeated him. Third, the desire for meaning may also result because individuals observe but are unable to understand or cope with an event which may become personally significant in the future. The advent of the Korean war, particularly to those of draft age and to those who were members of military reserve units, is a case in point. Cantril calls such situations *critical* and states that they comprise one of the general social and psycho-

---

[13] Hadley Cantril: *The Psychology of Social Movements*, New York, John Wiley & Sons, Inc., 1941, pp. 37–40.

logical conditions of suggestibility. In other words, in critical situations men will be inclined to accept the suggestions of leaders and propagandists if they seem to them to provide an adequate interpretation of the problems facing them.

Another condition of suggestibility arises from quite a different situation, namely one in which the individual's mental context is so rigidly fixed that a suggestion or stimulus is automatically judged by means of this context and with no critical examination of the stimulus or the suggestion itself.[14] In other words, the individual is suggestible because of his willingness to believe. For example, it is probable that a confirmed Communist will accept uncritically the interpretation of world events which is presented to him in the Communist party publications.

Thus, it is likely that the following of organizations that are either actively proposing or opposing social change consist of people who found meaningful the ideas presented by the leaders at a time when their previous mental contexts proved inadequate to solve the problems facing them. Furthermore, it is likely that followers who remain loyal to the organization even in the face of general social disapproval have allowed the ideology of the movement to become a fixed part of their general interpretation of life, so that they maintain a willingness to accept the suggestions offered by the leaders and the intellectuals. This does not preclude, of course, the possibility that sincere and critical thinkers may find the ideas of a group of leaders and intellectuals close enough to their own that they take a reasoned and mature part in the affairs of the organization.

Summary

Social change results from human interaction. The processes of human interaction which result in change are the same processes through which all social behavior is carried on. Among them are the conjunctive processes of cooperation, accommodation, and assimilation, and the disjunctive processes of competition and conflict.

Social change may be either purposeful or not. That which is not purposeful, which results from human interaction that is not explicitly directed toward change, can be called *sociocultural drift*. Social change which is purposeful, which results from human interaction definitely directed toward change, can be considered to be the result of social movements.

Such social movements may be characterized as either reformative or revolutionary in nature, the difference between these two being one of degree in terms of the scope of the aims of the movement and in terms of the degree to which the movements are accepted by the public.

The leadership of a social movement during its early stages is usually charismatic. The intelligentsia associated with it consists primarily of utopian thinkers. The leadership of organized opposition to social movements is also often charismatic. The intelligentsia associated with such opposition consists primarily of ideologic thinkers. The rank and file members of social movements and also of countermovements are primarily people who during critical situations in their lives found the ideologies

---

[14] *Ibid.*, pp. 62–75.

of the organization meaningful, and who have developed an intense will to believe in the interpretations of life offered by their leaders. Finally, since both social movements and their organized opposition are likely to go to extremes, the legitimate leadership of the society along with the more apathetic public and the uninvolved intelligentsia tend to be opposed to both groups.

chapter four

The Direction of Change
in the United States

One of the more difficult problems that we face in analyzing social change is that of determining and demonstrating its direction. Among the reasons for this difficulty is the fact that the meaning of the concept *direction* as applied to social change differs from the usual meaning of the term. Social change is extremely complex. It often seems to happen in an unplanned, random manner. We cannot properly speak of it running in a northerly or westerly direction like a river or a highway. Nor can we meaningfully describe it as moving up or down or left or right. We have no clear point of reference against which to measure it, save perhaps "now," in point of time. Even "now" is not a very clear reference point, for it itself is subject to constant change. "Now," for instance, is a good deal later on for the reader of this page than it is for the author.

Nevertheless, it is very important for us to know what changes are likely to occur in the future and how they are apt to affect our lives. We can arrive at such knowledge only if we can show that social change is a predictable process which proceeds in an understandable manner.

Since we have posited the agents of change developed in Chapter Two as the usual causal stimuli of social change, it follows that any directional patterns of social change are likely to derive from directional trends of those agents.

Patterns of Change of Agents of Change

Of the six categories of agents of change developed earlier, four—mechanical inventions, population movements, changes in natural resources, and the action of neighboring societies—seem to have the greatest effect upon contemporary American society at the present time. Our discussion of patterns of change will be limited to them.

Mechanical Invention

William F. Ogburn has studied extensively the patterns of change in material culture. He notes two basic patterns in the development of mechanical inventions. First, mechanical inventions tend to accumulate, so that the material culture becomes enlarged; and second, mechanical inventions become increasingly diversified and elaborated over the years.

33

Mechanical inventions tend to accumulate because a new artifact does not necessarily bring about the death of the artifact it replaces. Ogburn writes: "The use of bone is added to the use of stone. The use of bronze is added to the use of copper and the use of iron is added to the use of bronze. So that the stream of material culture grows bigger."[1] Cultural forms tend to persist, for even though new ways of doing things are invented, some people prefer to make use of the old and the familiar. The airliner has failed to eliminate the passenger train partly because some people do not want to fly. Furthermore, the new invention may not replace all of the functions of the old form. Thus, while the central heating plant of the modern home furnishes much more efficient heat than the old-fashioned fireplace, it does not replace the sentimental function of the hearth in the parlor; many homes nowadays are furnished with a fireplace, around which the family and its guests gather for discussions and recreation. Again, the tractor has not wholly supplanted the horse and the mule on American farms. Some fields cannot be economically worked with a tractor and the beast of burden remains a necessity.

However, as Ogburn writes, "Not all material culture is accumulative and not all forms persist. The record indeed shows that the use of some objects declines and the knowledge of making them is lost. For instance, we no longer chip flints to make stone implements for the chase . . ."[2] He goes on to warn against overemphasis on the accumulative nature of mechanical inventions, pointing out that over a long period of time many are lost because they cease to serve any function. Therefore the process of the accumulation of material aspects of culture can best be de-described as *selective accumulation*. That is, over the years many new inventions will be made and many old material forms discarded. The number of new inventions tends to exceed the number of discarded ones; hence there is in the long run a selective accumulation of material culture forms.

The elaboration and diversification of mechanical inventions can be attributed to the fact that a basic invention makes possible many various applications of its principle. For example, the development of the small gasoline-powered internal combustion engine made possible the derivation of many mechanisms driven by such power plants from the automobile to the "handy-billy" pump used aboard ship for supplementary water power, from the motorized bicycle to the gasoline-powered generator. The elaborations upon the internal combustion engine are seemingly countless, and their invention has probably not yet ceased.

One indication of the accumulation and elaboration of mechanical inventions is the activity of the United States Patent Office. Table 1 demonstrates a long term trend of increase in the number of patents issued for inventions.

Of course the mere listing of the numbers of patents issued is not too reliable an index of the number of mechanical inventions, for not every patent results in a usable machine. But these figures do provide some basis for judging the trend of our technological advance.

---

[1] William F. Ogburn: *Social Change*, New York, The Viking Press, 1950, p. 73.
[2] *Ibid.*, p. 75.

The processes of accumulation and elaboration seem to go by spurts set in motion by basic inventions. Periods of tremendous growth in the material culture followed such developments as the successful economic use of

TABLE 1

Patents Granted for Inventions by the
United States Patent Office, Selected
Years, 1845 to 1945*

Year	Number of Patents	Year	Number of Patents
1845	475	1895	20,883
1850	884	1900	24,660
1855	1,892	1905	29,784
1860	4,363	1910	35,168
1865	6,099	1915	43,207
1870	12,157	1920	37,164
1875	13,291	1925	46,450
1880	12,926	1930	45,243
1885	23,331	1935	40,683
1890	25,322	1940	42,333
		1945	25,719

* Bureau of the Census, Historical Statistics of the United States, 1789–1945, Series P 177, U.S. Department of Commerce, 1949.

steam as a source of power and the invention of the gasoline-powered internal combustion engine. The discovery of atomic energy and inventions for its application as well as the invention of plastics also seem to be basic in nature and promise a new era of rapid expansion of the technological aspects of life in the future.

Population Movements

Population movement is perhaps the most easily measured and described of any of the important agents of change, for the United States Census provides a wealth of data. Among the more important aspects of demographic change for which data are available are changes in population size, change in composition—both in culture groups and in age structure—and change in the spatial distribution of the population.

The population of the United States has been growing ever since the country was founded. Table 2 presents the total population of the United States by decade from 1850 until 1950 together with the percentage increase over the total population of the previous decade.

A glance at Table 2 indicates that although population has increased considerably each decade, it has not increased as much during recent decades as it did during the last half of the nineteenth century. This decline in the rate of increase results from the fact that our birth rate has, generally speaking, declined as our population has become better educated and more concentrated in cities. However, the declining birth rate has been more than compensated for by a rapidly declining death rate so that while fewer babies are being born per family now than were being born fifty years ago, even fewer people, especially infants, are dying. The severe restrictions on immigration instituted in 1924 have also contributed to the decreasing rate of population growth that the United States has experienced since then.

TABLE 2

Total United States Population and Percentage Increase of Population by Decade from
1850 to 1950*

Year	Total Population	Percentage Increase over Previous Decade
1850	23,191,876	26.4
1860	31,443,321	26.2
1870	38,558,371	18.5
1880	50,155,783	23.1
1890	62,947,714	20.3
1900	75,994,575	17.2
1910	91,972,266	17.4
1920	105,710,620	13.0
1930	122,775,046	13.9
1940	131,669,275	6.6
1950	150,697,361	12.6

* Bureau of the Census, *Statistical Abstract of the United States, 1953,* U.S. Department of Commerce, Table 10.

Another aspect of our population which has changed during the course of our history is the cultural background of the groups which make up our total population. The United States was settled primarily by people who were born in northern European countries, and Anglo-Saxon culture provided the basis upon which the culture of the United States was built.

TABLE 3

Immigrants Admitted from All Countries
Representative Years, 1820 to 1951*

Year	Number	Year	Number
1820	8,385	1910	1,041,570
1830	23,322	1915	326,700
1840	84,066	1920	430,001
1850	369,980	1925	204,314
1860	153,640	1930	241,700
1870	387,203	1935	34,956
1880	457,257	1940	70,756
1890	455,302	1945	38,119
1900	448,572	1950	249,187
1905	1,026,499	1951	205,717

* Bureau of the Census, *Historical Statistics of the United States, 1789–1945,* Series B 304, and *Statistical Abstract of the United States, 1952,* U.S. Department of Commerce, Table 105.

From about 1820 until about 1880 most of the immigrants were people of northern European stock with cultural background similar to those who had already become dominant in our society. Those migrants are often referred to as the "old immigration," consisting primarily of northern European families, many of whom came to settle the agricultural land on the American frontier. During the decade prior to 1880 the character of the people coming into the United States changed greatly, as did the volume of immigration. By 1880 an increasing percentage of our immigrants came from the southern and eastern parts of Europe, which meant that they contrasted sharply in cultural background with the people already resident in the United States. This "new immigration" found the frontiers of America already settled, and hence it provided the United States with an urban rather than a rural population, although most of the new immigrants were of peasant background. The numbers entering the United States around the turn of the twentieth century grew to gigantic proportions; the years 1905, 1906, 1907, 1910, 1913, and 1914 found more than one million people coming to our shores, and most of these settled in cities, supporting themselves by unskilled industrial labor. After 1924 when the quota system was installed and the numbers of immigrants coming from southern and eastern Europe was severely restricted, the tide of new residents was stemmed. From 1931 until 1945, we received less than 100,000 immigrants each year. In 1933 the number dropped to 23,068. (See Table 3.)

The population of the United States is also changing in terms of the age-group composition. The declining birth rate and the more rapidly declining death rate have resulted in an increase of the average age of our citizenry. Table 4 compares the percentage distribution of the population of the United States by age group in 1880 with that in 1950.

TABLE 4

*Percentage Distribution by Age of the Population
of the United States, 1880 and 1950**

Year	Under 10	10–19	20–29	30–39	40–49	50–64	Over 65
1950	19.5	14.4	15.7	15.1	12.8	14.3	8.1
1880	26.7	21.4	18.3	12.7	9.1	8.4	3.4

* Warren S. Thompson: *Population Problems*, New York, McGraw-Hill Book Company, Inc, 1953, p. 95. Used by permission.

The figures in Table 4 demonstrate the long-term trend of change in the age distribution of our population. Our population is growing older; there is a greater proportion of people over thirty and a smaller proportion of people under thirty than there were seventy years ago. However, important minor trends also occur which may either accelerate or even reverse this process for comparatively short lengths of time. For instance, during the depression of the 1930s the birth rate dropped greatly and the process of aging of our population was comparatively quickened. On the other hand, since the beginning of World War II there has been a sizable increase in birth rate, making for a reversal of the population trend, with the average age of the population growing somewhat younger.

Another type of population change is related to the patterns of internal migration within the country. The direction of such internal migration during the twentieth century has been as follows: people brought up on farms have tended to move to urban areas, particularly those urban areas which have developed on the western and southwestern edges of our country. Recently many rural southerners have been moving north and west to industrial cities and many midwesterners have been moving to the west coast cities. Except for depression years, when the process has been reversed in part, rural areas of our country have always lost population, and the urban areas of our country have tended to gain population, in comparison with the over-all increase of population.

Natural Resources

Five basic trends of change in the natural resources of the United States deserve stress. In the first place, we are experiencing the depletion of many of the raw materials of our economic system. The effects of this trend have been somewhat mitigated by four other trends which tend to extend the life of our resources—the invention of ways to utilize low-grade materials and substitutes, the utilization of completely new resources, the growth of sources of supply external to the United States, and the development of sound conservation policies.

Among the many raw materials which have been seriously depleted are timber, topsoil, and high-grade iron ores. Fifty per cent more saw timber is cut each year than is grown. This means that a continuation of this rate will seriously deplete our reserves of timber for building purposes in the near future.[3] As the saw timber has been logged off, the lumber industry has moved from old forests into new ones. The focus of logging has followed the movement of the population of the United States from east to west. Maine was the major logging state of the first half of the nineteenth century. New York's logging industry was at its peak in the 1850s and the 1860s. Pennsylvania was the great lumber state of the 1870s; Michigan in the 1880s; Wisconsin in the 1890s; Minnesota in the first decade of the twentieth century. Now the greatest logging operations are carried on in the Pacific Northwest, western Canada, and southern Alaska.[4]

The nation has all too recently experienced the results of overgrazing, overplowing, and underplanting in the areas of the southwest where the dustbowl (dramatized by John Steinbeck in his novel, *The Grapes of Wrath*) plagued the inhabitants of that region during the 1930s. And although the proximity of high-grade iron ore to great coal deposits provided the basis for the immense industrial development of the United States, we are experiencing depletion in this area too, for some of our high-grade iron ore deposits are running low. The greatest high-grade ore producing area, the Mesabi Range, is not likely to remain in production more than another

---

[3] C. Edward Behre: "Forest Land and Timber Resources," in *Trees, the Yearbook of Agriculture, 1949*, U.S. Dept. of Agriculture, Washington, D.C. Government Printing Office, pp. 715–721.

[4] George T. Renner, Loyal Durand, Jr., G. Langdon White, and Weldon B. Gibson: *World Economic Geography: An Introduction to Geonomics*, New York, Thomas Y. Crowell Co., 1951, p. 294.

twenty years,[5] and we are finding it necessary to develop resources outside our own country, particularly in Labrador and Quebec, where large, untapped resources are available.

The picture is not entirely gloomy, however, for the United States abounds in low-grade ores, and there has been considerable development of ways to utilize them economically. Similarly, as the pinch for any metal becomes very great, methods of re-use are developed or substitutes found. The development of such techniques constitutes a countertrend to the depletion of our resources.

New resources, particularly new fuels, have been intensively developed during the past half century. The immense proliferation of petroleum products is an example, as is the growth in importance of radioactive materials for the production of atomic energy. As such, the development of new resources constitutes an important trend which mitigates the depletion of other resources.

Luckily for us, our immediate neighbors, Mexico and Canada, are able to supply us with many of the resources which are disappearing in the United States. One of the ways in which we have made up for our losses and for the excess of our needs over our ability to produce has been to enter into agreements with these and other nations by which we import raw materials necessary to our economic system. Therefore, a third trend which compensates for the depletion of our natural resources is our increasing use of resources found outside our own borders.

Finally, there has been the growth of sound conservation policies. These policies have represented a modification of our values of individualism, for they have required considerable governmental control and considerable cooperation among groups and individuals who are in economic competition with one another. The rise of conservation practices in agriculture, lumbering, and other extractive industries has been a rather recent phenomenon, not really getting under way until the 1930s. Nevertheless, it represents what is probably the most important trend which has taken place in response to the threat of the depletion of our resources.

The Action of Neighboring Societies

The fourth important agent of change, the effect of neighboring societies upon us, has increased in importance each year. With the development of rapid communication, horribly efficient weapons of warfare, and our increased dependence upon sources outside our borders for raw materials, our lives have become inextricably entwined with the lives of others, and our destiny has increasingly been determined by our relations with foreign countries.

The twentieth century has been a century of struggle. Conflicting economic systems, national ambitions, and political viewpoints have made international crisis the normal state of affairs; this condition shows every sign of continuing. During the century as America's political influence, economic importance, and military power have grown she has been involved in world wars, depressions, international inflation, and finally, in an over-

---

[5] *Ibid.*, p. 403.

seas police action and a cold war. She has found herself in the position of being a principal champion of democracy in the world-wide struggle against totalitarianism.

For the individual American citizen, these events seem to have led to a sense of insecurity, and many of the reactions of the public have indicated continuing and growing anxieties. It is perhaps ironical that even as America's political and military power has grown tremendously, the American public seems to have lost its faith in its power to determine its own fate; nevertheless, this fact has determined many of the changes which have taken place in our society.

Basic Trends of Social Change in America

The directional trends observed above in the four most important agents of change have resulted in basic patterns of change in the institutional structure of American society. Taken over-all, the general direction has been toward an increase in urbanism as a way of life and toward an increase in bureaucracy as a method of administration and organization.

Urbanization

The concept of the process of urbanization is related to the idea of a continuum extending from "simple" rural or folk society at one extreme to the modern complex urban society at the other.

Robert Redfield and Louis Wirth have written complementary articles presenting ideal types of folk society and urban society, respectively. Redfield describes the folk society as a small, isolated one in which intimacy typifies relations among the members, in which there is not much division of social and economic labor, and which is marked by a very slow rate of social change. He writes:

> Thus, we may characterize the folk society as small, isolated, non-literate, and homogeneous with a strong sense of group solidarity . . . The members of the folk society are guided in acting by previously established comprehensive and interdependent conventional understanding; at any one time they do many different things, which are complexly related to one another to express collective sentiments and conceptions . . . We may say, then, that in the folk society, conventional behavior is strongly patterned; it tends to conform to a type or a norm . . . We may still further say that the patterns of what people think should be done are closely consistent with what they believe is done, and that there is one way, or a very few conventional ways, in which everybody has some understanding and some share in meeting each need that arises.[6]

Louis Wirth points out that the characterization of the community as urban on the basis of size alone is arbitrary. He depicts the typical large city as containing a great range of individual variation, noting that competition and formal control mechanisms furnish substitutes for the primary group solidarity that holds the folk society together. There is a great heterogeneity of population when the roles played by individuals tend to become specialized and highly segmental. The city is marked by the proliferation

---

[6] Robert Redfield: "The Folk Society," *American Journal of Sociology* 52:293-308 (1947). Used by permission.

of secondary contacts, and this leads to the "sophistication" and rationality generally ascribed to members of urban societies. There are no effective extended kinship ties; the community and the formal voluntary association function as fictional "kinship" groups to which loyalty is rationally given by their members.[7]

With these traits in mind, it can be recognized that urbanization means more than the fact that cities are growing and that a greater and greater percentage of our population is living in or near them. Rather, as a basic trend of social change, urbanization refers to the fact that the society as a whole is becoming more and more citylike. Our social institutions are increasingly based upon the modes of behavior necessary for life in a cosmopolitan, mobile, heterogeneous, materialistic, rational, and secondary society; our folkways and mores are less and less determined by what is traditional, by primary association, by considerations of a sacred nature, by a homogeneous society. And we shall see that this basic trend applies to each of our major social institutions; that it is perhaps true that not only we in America, but the world as a whole is becoming increasingly urbanized, and that urbanization as a process of change is rapidly gaining momentum.

The process of urbanization is largely a product of the directional trends of the agents of change discussed earlier in this chapter. The development of mechanical inventions leads to greater industrialization, more rapid and efficient transportation and communication, and an increasing emphasis on material goods in our society. Population growth results in a larger and hence more densely settled population. Internal migration distributes an increasing proportion of population in metropolitan areas. Changes in our natural resources necessitate greater dependence on foreign lands. The press of world events makes us take a larger and larger part in world affairs, and we become less and less isolationistic. All of these factors contribute to the gaining momentum of urbanization in all aspects of American life, and because of them, the processes are very likely to continue unabated in the future, unless a truly violent reversal of the trends of change of the agents of change takes place.

Bureaucratization

Bureaucracy is characteristically associated with urbanism. Bureaucracy as defined by Max Weber, the social theorist who has made the greatest contribution to its understanding, is a system of management of either public or private formal associations. It is to be contrasted with management which is personal, patriarchal, or paternal in nature. Weber develops the following characteristics of the ideal bureaucracy:

1. A bureau consists of a series of integrated offices, each with its fixed and official duties.

2. Positions within the offices are strictly graded as to status and authority, and the holders of the lower positions are supervised by higher officials. Because of this, there is always the possibility that a client may appeal a decision made by a lesser official to higher ones, following the "chain of command."

3. In principle, the business of the bureau is always carried on in the same

---

[7] Louis Wirth: "Urbanism as a Way of Life," *American Journal of Sociology* 44:1–24 (1938).

way regardless of the personality of the office holder and regardless of the prestige of the client. All transactions are reported in writing, and these reports are carefully checked and filed.

4. Ideally, the officials are fully trained and experienced to the degree required by the office.

5. The officials follow relatively general, stable, and exhaustive rules in accomplishing their work. Knowledge of these rules constitutes a special technical learning which the office holders must possess.[8]

The management of public and private organizations by means of this ordered, hierarchical, specialized, and, to some extent, professional type of organization makes for an office holder who, according to Weber, most typically is professionally oriented to a career within the bureaucracy, who enjoys a social esteem based upon his rank in the hierarchy in which he serves, who is appointed on the basis of his skill, his experience, and his training rather than on the basis of whom he knows or to whom he is related, whose tenure is guaranteed as long as he obeys the rules of bureaucratic management, who expects advancement up the hierarchical ladder within the office. Characteristically the bureaucrat is a man who thinks "by the book," to whom the rules of the office often become practically sacred, but for whom the rules are set up with a specific, rational purpose in mind.

The development of bureaucracy is associated with the growth of a money economy and is signaled by the rise of huge and complex organizations. In fact, huge organizations handling millions of dollars probably could not be managed in any manner other than bureaucratically. Imagine the chaos that would exist if the amount of postage required for a letter or a parcel were to be determined on each occasion by means of bargaining between the customer and the postal clerk. What if Western Union routed its telegrams according to the whims of the operators along the way? Life at General Motors would certainly be ridiculous if every member of the managerial and office forces felt it necessary to impress personally the president of the company in order to obtain a promotion. Such organizations must be set up on a detached and impersonal basis, if they are to function at all. Lines of communication and chains of command must be understood by all concerned. The officers of the concern must be able to count on jobs being accomplished in a predictable manner, whoever the individuals doing the job happen to be. Rewards must be distributed rationally if the morale of the staff is to be maintained. All of these factors necessitate a bureaucratic setup, and therefore any complex organization inevitably becomes bureaucratized.

The process of bureaucratization, then, does not refer merely to well-known developments in government, but applies to every aspect of life which is characterized by social organizations which are large and complex. That is to say, the growth of ordered, hierarchical, specialized, and professional management is to be found in the church, in science, in government, in business, in education, in both amateur and professional sport, in

---

[8] Cf. Max Weber: "Bureaucracy," Chapter VIII of *From Max Weber: Essays in Sociology*. Translated and edited by H. H. Gerth and C. Wright Mills. New York, Oxford University Press, 1946, pp. 196–198.

entertainment. The process of necessity has been accompanied by a modification in our values of rugged individualism and by a relative loss of status of the individual entrepreneur. Nowadays, the popular idea of the self-made man is one who started out as stock clerk and finally became first vice-president of the company, rather than the merchant who expanded his pushcart to a chain of stores wholly owned by himself.

The process of bureaucratization as a major direction of social change, like urbanization, results from the changes taking place in the agents of change discussed earlier in this chapter. As the development of mechanical invention leads to greater size and diversification of our industrial organizations; as the population grows older and therefore gains an increasing orientation toward security rather than individual enterprise; as our whole life becomes more involved in international relations, our typical patterns of social organization are becoming more and more like the ideal typical bureaucracy that Weber described. Unless there is a considerable reversal of these trends in the future, it is likely that the process of bureaucratization will continue unabated.

The Direction of Change in American Social Institutions

Let us now look at the changes which have occurred and are occurring in each of the basic social institutions with which we are concerned.

The Family

Urbanization and bureaucratization are each reflected in the changing American family today. As the country has become more urbanized the American family has lost many of its earlier functions. It typically has fewer members, its activities are much more scattered, it lives in much smaller quarters, and its internal control is much more democratic.

In early America the family was characteristically located in a semi-isolated rural setting, and was therefore dependent upon itself for recreation, economic endeavor, education, and religious worship. Nowadays these functions are taken care of outside of the home by specialized organizations, often by large-scale bureaucracies.

As the American family has left the farm and settled in the city, large numbers of children have ceased to be an economic asset and have to a large extent become quite an expensive economic liability. For the urban family each child means another mouth to feed and another room to rent—to be paid from the relatively fixed income of the parents, whereas back on the farm each new child became after a few years virtually a low-paid farmhand, adding his share to the family income.

The rural family of early America was usually semipatriarchal, as was the typical family of many of the immigrant groups which have come to America more recently. But nowadays the patriarchal pattern has broken down as women with their growing status in urbanized society have taken an increasing share of the control of the family.

While the family has lost many of its original functions, it has gained some new ones. The anonymity of urbanism and the impersonal nature of bureaucracy have resulted in the fact that many of the individual needs for recognition, a feeling of purposefulness, and for the expression of creativity are no longer satisfied in the economic life of many people. Therefore many have turned to the family for satisfaction in these areas. It is likely that such aspects of life as the care and training of children and the decoration and upkeep of the home are increasingly becoming a major concern of American husbands and fathers. It is also probable that the spending habits of the family, the quality of the household furnishings, and the like play a growing part in the display of status in the life of modern Americans.

The Government

The American governmental pattern was originally developed for a rural, largely agricultural nation, in which transportation facilities were limited, and in which regional differences tended to be extreme. Towns and townships were often governed in principle by means of the direct participation of the electorate in town meetings. The emphasis of the men who first set up the state and national governments was upon a maximum of local control and a minimum of centralized power.

As America has become urbanized and has grown in size, population, power, and complexity, new needs have arisen and we have altered our original pattern of government little by little. The power of the federal government has grown immensely. Local governmental units have also increased their functions but have steadily lost power in comparison to the federal government.

Problems have arisen in various areas of our life, and through the years various men and parties seeking political power have suggested governmental programs to mitigate them. Thus government has extended itself into fields previously covered by economic agencies, the school, the medical profession, the church, and many others.

As government has grown in power, size, and complexity it has, of course, become increasingly bureaucratized. The process of bureaucratization is exemplified by the increasing use of civil service and the decreasing use of patronage in filling government jobs on all levels, and although this aspect of bureaucratization suffers temporary reverses now and then, a greater and greater proportion of the growing number of governmental employees are chosen and promoted on the basis of objective tests of their merit.

Not only has urbanization contributed to the growth of governmental size, power, and complexity and hence to the growth of bureaucracy, but it has also helped to create some problems of government which are as yet unsolved. This is particularly true of municipal governments. As cities have grown and metropolitan areas have developed the urban population of many of them has spilled over into unincorporated areas and surrounded incorporated towns. As a result, many metropolitan districts are almost hopelessly entangled in an uncoordinated web of conflicting local authorities. For instance, in 1951 within the metropolitan district of St. Louis there were 5 counties, 18 townships, more than 100 municipalities, at least 425 school districts, and 21 special districts—more than 560 separate governmental units.[9] The cost of duplicated functions and lack of efficient cooperation must be very great indeed.

[9] Stuart A. Queen, and David B. Carpenter: *The American City*, New York, McGraw-Hill Book Company, Inc., 1953, p. 307.

The Economic System

The economic system is perhaps the social institution which is most prone to change, for it is exceedingly sensitive to such agents of change as mechanical inventions, population movements, and changes in natural resources. Therefore it has greatly influenced changes in other social institutions. For instance, the development of an industrial economy has been in large part responsible for the loss of family functions. The dislocations associated with the business cycle—the pattern of alternate inflations and depressions which has in the past characterized our economy—are primarily responsible for the increased control over business by the government, and hence for the increase in the complexity of government.

The dominant pattern of change of the economic system is one of collectivization and centralization. This pattern appears throughout the economy—in agriculture, in retailing, in manufacture, in communications, and in labor unions. The individual entrepreneur (although as numerous as ever in our history), the small craft union, the family farm, and the master craftsman in his little shop are all declining in relative importance as compared to the giant corporation, the government owned or controlled monopoly, the giant-scale mechanized farm, the large industrial union, and the assembly line.

This pattern reflects the trends of urbanization and bureaucratization in that its development is dependent upon the existence of a mass market and upon scientific, rational, and impersonal management.

Religion

When America was a land of rural communities, the church tended to be the focal point of the social life of the town. The people in most small villages or towns were relatively homogeneous in their religious, as well as other, interests. There were seldom more than two or three different churches in a single community, for rarely was there need for more. Nowadays, as America has become more urbanized, there is a greater diversity of forms of religious worship because the populations of most communities are quite heterogeneous. With the decline of personal social control, religious organizations have had to rely increasingly upon their ability to appeal to the needs of their members, for social pressure does not as readily force apathetic people to church on the Sabbath. Because the need to appeal to diverse interests is felt more intensely each year, churches employ trained personnel to do special jobs. Experts on education, recreation, publication, and theology are becoming more important in the increasingly bureaucratized religious organizations of America. Even those denominations which emphasize the ministry of all Christians have tended to expand the educational requirements for placement in pastoral positions, and the keynote of today's clergy is *training*.

Among the results of the growth of bureaucracy in the church is the growth of social distance between the minister, who increasingly plays the role of official, and his flock, who are becoming more and more like the clients of any bureaucratic organization. The congregations nowadays often appear to take on the role of spectatorship rather than of active participation.[10]

The bureaucratization of the major American churches has helped to give rise to a reaction in the form of intensely personal, loosely organized sects, typically appealing to the lower socioeconomic status groups. Although the turnover of the membership of these groups is large, the great number of them, to be found occupying abandoned commercial buildings in the poorer urban neighborhoods and shacks in rural communities, attests to the need felt by many Americans for a type of religion which offers them emotional release and the feeling that they as individuals are in direct contact with a deity personally interested in them.

Science

In a recent article in the *New Yorker* Dr. Samuel A. Goldschmit, chairman of the Physics Department of the Brookhaven National Laboratory, was quoted as decrying the passing of the "string and sealing wax" era of physics.[11] Dr. Goldschmit was contrasting the present era of well-financed, high-prestige research centers devoted to the physical sciences with the era before World War II, when many physicists worked in makeshift laboratories in forgotten corners of a few university campuses.

The traditional concept of the scientist working as an individual, scrounging for funds, receiving reward only in personal satisfaction and in the esteem of a few colleagues is rapidly changing. While this image was never completely accurate, it is true that nowadays fewer and fewer basic problems are solved by individuals working alone in private laboratories. Science, like business and government, is becoming collectivized, bureaucratized, and heavily subsidized. Business and government have found it necessary to utilize the scientists, and in so doing they have provided them with well-equipped laboratories which are best worked by teams of specialists. And most scientists now receive rewards in terms of high salaries and considerable social prestige. This fact worries some scientists because they fear that concentration upon planned research by a team of specialists may result in missing the lucky breaks and flashes of insight which have played a large part in basic invention and discovery.

Education

With the bureaucratization of business, industry, and government, education has become more than ever a marketable commodity. Formal educational requirements are specified for a greater number of positions in all of these walks of life, for employers must be assured that the people they hire are competent to deal with the complexities of their jobs. The broader need for education coupled with the growing ability of an expanding and more densely settled population to pay for education has made for the evolution of large, centralized educational systems which have large student bodies.

[10] Charles H. Page: "Bureaucracy and the Liberal Church," *Review of Religion*, March, 1952, pp. 147–149.

[11] Daniel Lang: "A Farewell to String and Sealing Wax," *New Yorker*, Vol. XXIX, No. 38 (November 7, 1953), p. 47.

Not only is education expanding, but it is becoming increasingly specialized and more intensely oriented toward specific vocational goals. Students no longer receive as a matter of course training in Greek, Latin, or philosophy in most schools. Rather, more and more students are vocationally or professionally trained in practical subjects. Because many educators feel that overspecialization may make for an uninformed, easily misled citizenry, there has arisen a countertrend in which the emphasis is on core-curriculum, or general education which attempts to guarantee that the vocational or professional student will receive sufficient training outside his specialty to be an intelligent, useful, and happy citizen.

Meanwhile, as educational systems have grown and specialized they have themselves become bureaucratic, and have become wedded to guaranteed salary schedules, merit raises, competitive examinations for position and promotion, specific educational requirements for employees, and the like. These developments have made teaching as a profession attractive to those who crave security, and have resulted in a teaching force which is, by and large, quite competent and well trained. Unfortunately, however, bureaucracy carries with it penalties in the form of a growing unwillingness to innovate or to tamper with what has become established routine. Bureaucratization nearly always implies standardization, rigidity, and often mediocrity. In a recent Broadway production which satirized modern civilization, a character who was supposed to be the epitome of the present-day corporation executive remarked, "What we need is a standardized working-man with interchangeable parts." There are those who fear that modern, bureaucratic education will soon be turning out a product that fits those specifications.

Recreation

Recreation reflects the urbanization and bureaucratization of America, especially apparent in the developmental trends of commercialization and the growth of public and philanthropic recreational programs.

Taken as a whole, recreation is a giant industry. Americans spend many millions of dollars each year on motion pictures, commercial radio and television, books, magazines, night clubs, professional athletics, and organized vice. The growth of commercial recreation reflects the decline of the recreational functions of the home, and also the increase of leisure time.

With the decline of family recreation and the parallel growth of leisure, social problems such as delinquency, excessive drinking, and gambling have arisen. Government, in response, has entered the recreational field, as witnessed by the recent growth of public programs of organized play. Parks are owned and maintained by most major governmental units. Trained recreation directors are employed by many agencies to organize team play in various sports and games, and to supervise dances, outings, and playgrounds.

In addition, many industries have developed recreational programs for their employees, in an effort not only to maintain their physical and mental health but to reduce the hostility of employees toward the employers. Philanthropic agencies such as the YMCA, YWCA, and various community centers have also developed recreational programs to help train children to be effective citizens and in order to help curb delinquency.

Summary

The basic institutions of American life have undergone change by which they have become more urbanized and more bureaucratized. Urbanization and bureaucratization have resulted from the pressures put on the institutional structure by certain overwhelming events, particularly those which can be classified as mechanical inventions, population movements, changes in natural resources, and the effects of the actions of neighboring societies. These agents of change tend to create dysfunctions in one or another aspect of the institutional structure so that human needs go unmet, thus necessitating change in order to meet those needs. The resulting social change is carried out by human beings as they interact with one another. Most change is not purposefully carried out but rather is the result of sociocultural drift, as people adjust their ways of thinking, doing, and feeling in order to meet new situations. However, sometimes dissatisfactions and tensions become sufficiently acute so that people are motivated to take direct and positive action to remove them. In such cases, people often respond to charismatic leadership and utopian ideologies in various social movements.

Change in any aspect of the institutional structure, no matter how it comes about, often gives rise to dysfunctions in other segments, necessitating further change, so that waves of social change, once started, tend to be self-perpetuating. Thus, the directional trends we have observed are likely to continue in the future.

This discussion of social change has, of course, been limited in scope. It is hoped that it has been successful in bringing out some of the basic processes of change as they affect American society. However, an outline only has been attempted. The reader is referred to the selected readings that follow for more complete discussions of the various aspects of the field.

Selected Readings

BLUMER, HERBERT: "Collective Behavior" in Lee, Alfred McClung (ed.): *New Outline of the Principles of Sociology*, Part IV, New York, Barnes & Noble, Inc., 1946.
Blumer's theory of social movements (employed in Chapter Three of this study) is here presented in brief form.

CANTRIL, HADLEY: *The Psychology of Social Movements*, New York, John Wiley & Sons, Inc., 1941.
This is an attempt to develop a sound social-psychological theory of social movements; Part II contains interesting case studies of movements in the United States and elsewhere.

CHINOY, ELY: *Sociological Perspective: Basic Concepts and Their Application* (Studies in Sociology), New York, Random House, Inc., 1954.
Among other concepts treated in this study are culture, institution, societal types, function and dysfunction, stability and change, and equilibrium—all important tools in the analysis of social change.

HATT, PAUL K., and ALBERT J. REISS, JR. (eds.): *Reader in Urban Sociology*, Glencoe, Ill., The Free Press, 1951.
Perhaps the best collection of readings on modern urbanization. Changing population structure is treated in Part V and changing social institutions in Part VII.

HERMAN, ABBOTT P.: *An Approach to Social Problems*, Boston, Ginn & Company, 1949.
Herman discusses with insight the relation of social problems and social change; the overwhelming event as an agent of social change is fully developed.

MACIVER, ROBERT M., and CHARLES H. PAGE: *Society, An Introductory Analysis*, New York, Rinehart & Company, Inc., 1949, Book Three, "Social Change."
This work presents a theoretical discussion of social change and its relation to biophysical, cultural, and technological aspects of life. The focus is larger than this study's and the viewpoint is different though not opposing. An excellent bibliography is included.

MANNHEIM, KARL: *Ideology and Utopia: An Introduction to the Sociology of Knowledge*, New York, Harcourt, Brace & Co., 1936.
————: *Man and Society in an Age of Reconstruction*, New York, Harcourt, Brace & Co., 1940.
The first volume is a pioneer work on the role of the intellectual in social change; the second is a theoretically sophisticated interpretation of changes in Western society during recent decades.

MERTON, ROBERT K.: *Social Theory and Social Structure*, Glencoe, Ill., The Free Press, 1949.
Chapter 1 of this influential work analyzes manifest and latent functions, including their relation to change; Chapters 5 and 6 consider problems of bureaucracy; Chapters 8 and 9 treat the sociology of knowledge, and 11 through 15 the sociology of science. A required reading for the serious student of any of these topics.

MERTON, ROBERT K., et al. (eds.): *Reader in Bureaucracy*, Glencoe, Ill., The Free Press, 1952.
An excellent collection of readings on the nature, growth, advantages, and problems of bureaucracy; with a useful bibliography.

OGBURN, WILLIAM F.: *Social Change*, New York, The Viking Press, Inc., 1922 and 1950.
The 1950 edition is a revision of this influential study in which the hypothesis of cultural lag is presented.

WEBER, MAX: *From Max Weber: Essays in Sociology*. Edited and translated by H. H. Gerth and C. W. Mills. New York, Oxford University Press, Inc., 1946.
   The introductory comments by Gerth and Mills on Weber's treatment of bureaucracy and charisma are valuable; their translation of Weber's essays on these and other subjects adds enormously to suggestive social theory available to the English reader.
WILLIAMS, ROBIN M., JR.: *American Society, A Sociological Interpretation*, New York, Alfred A. Knopf, Inc., 1951.
   A keen analysis of social and cultural structure of the United States, including, especially in Chapters 11, 13, and 14, a consideration of stability, integration, and change in our society.
WILSON, LOGAN, and WILLIAM L. KOLB: *Sociological Analysis*, New York, Harcourt, Brace & Co., 1949.
   In Chapters 20 and 21 the editors provide a general discussion of conjunctive and disjunctive social processes, followed by six articles on different phases of these subjects. Chapter 23 is concerned with various aspects of contemporary social change, including the role of social movements.